MW01110119

Marriage Coaching

Heart, Hope & Skills for a Great Relationship

Jeff & Jill Williams

Foreword by Tony Stoltzfus

Copyright © 2011 by Jeffrey J. Williams. All rights reserved.
Marriage Coaching: Heart, Hope and Skills for a Great Relationship
Published by Grace & Truth Relationship Education, LLC
Springfield, Ohio 45503

No part of this publication may be reproduced, stored in a retrieval system or
transmitted in any form or by any means, electronic, mechanical, photocopying,
recording, scanning or otherwise without the prior written permission of the Author.
Requests to the Author for permission should be addressed to:

Grace & Truth Relationship Education, LLC,
3137 Campbell Drive, Springfield, Ohio 45503.
E-mail: jeff.gtre@gmail.com, or marriagecoaches@gmail.com
Call: 937-717-5591 (United States)
Printed in the United States of America

ISBN 978-1468000801
First Edition: December 2011

Editorial Services Provided by David Yeazell,
P.O. Box 383194, Duncanville, TX 75138; info@yeazellconsulting.com.

Graphic Design Services Provided by Michael Cartwright
cartwrightdesign@gmail.com

Unless otherwise notes, all scripture references are from THE HOLY BIBLE,
NEW INTERNATIONAL VERSION®, NIV® Copyright © 1973, 1978, 1984,
2011 by Biblica, Inc.™ Used by permission. All rights reserved worldwide.

Certain individuals mentioned as clients are real but have had their names changed.
Other individuals mentioned by name as clients are composite characters. Any
resemblance to real people is completely accidental.

*We dedicate Marriage Coaching to Jeff's parents,
John (1940-2011) and Pat Williams. Thank you for loving and
believing in us. Our family story is the fuel of our passion to heal,
strengthen and protect marriages and families.*

Love, Jeff and Jill

Endorsements

Marriage Coaching reflects the author's extensive knowledge and long experience in the emerging and growing field of coaching by outlining practical methods for self-coaching in marriages and guidelines for those who might want to coach other couples. Written from a Christian, biblical perspective by authors who are experienced and knowledgeable in their craft, it is a unique book – practical, relevant, readable, innovative, personal and biblical. If you want to coach others in their marriages or coach your own marriage, this is the book that will be your guide. I am happy to endorse it enthusiastically.

Gary R. Collins, PhD
Former President of The American Association of Christian Counseling and author of more than 50 books, including *Christian Counseling: A Comprehensive Guide, The Biblical Basis of Christian Counseling*, and *Christian Coaching: Helping Others Turn Potential into Reality*

Jeff and Jill Williams are battle scarred veterans whose decades of Christian service have molded them into compassionate helpers of those in need. Over the decades they [have] assisted many hundreds of couples [to] resolve seemingly intractable conflicts and commit to loving, honoring and respecting one another. As marriage coaches they've heard every excuse from couples ready to give up and split up. But through the Holy Spirit's presence and power, many once barren hearts have blossomed with hope, faith and love.

How does this happen so frequently? The focus of Jeff and Jill's new book is straight forward. Their coaching model focuses on the couple, their strengths and willingness to work together for mutual benefit. Why encourage couples to coach each other rather than see a marriage counselor? Simply put: Most couples wait until it too late before seeking help. Marriage coaching focuses on the positives present in relationships rather than the negatives. It's a cup more than half full approach rather than a problem focused approach. It's a proactive preventative approach to better marriages. The positive nature of this model builds skills and forms positive attitudes from the start.

Marriage Coaching is a must read for every couple. Why? None of us have it all together and all of us will benefit from the wisdom and strategies Jeff and Jill have penned.

Dr. Alan N. Keiran
Captain, Chaplain Corps, US Navy (ret.)
Chief of Staff, Office of the U.S. Senate Chaplain
President, Dunamis International Ministries
Author: *Take Charge of Your Destiny and Don't Be Surprised*

As a ministry, the Waterboyz for Jesus saw that one of the major obstacles to raising up godly men were relationship busters. We realized that when our relationships are in crisis the enemy has cut our hair and poked our eyes out just like he did with Samson.

Jeff 'happened' to appear at an event just in time to assist one of the men who had reached a crisis in his marriage. Jeff and Jill stepped into this marriage crisis while inviting my wife and I to tag along to observe. What we saw over the next several weeks was a unique and powerful way of offering a rescue. Jeannie and I were so impressed we immediately signed up for their coaching class. My marriage has never been the same. We continue to use many of the tools and techniques we learned during this training, in our marriage and helping other couples in crisis.

Jeff and Jill have a unique way of transparently inviting you into their own personal story as a way of modeling the skills they teach. They have an uncommon way of getting communication started, holding hope for struggling couples, and casting a compelling God view of a potential marriage rescue. If you want your marriage to be more, if you find yourself battling for marriage reconciliation, then take the time to read this book. More than that invest in putting into practice the things you learn. This book will be a great addition to your marriage, ministry, and Kingdom potential. Besides, you'll laugh, you'll cry, and you'll breathe the air of the Kingdom. So hang on and enjoy the ride!

Paul Foss
President, Waterboyz for Jesus
www.waterboyz.org

The skills and mindsets offered by Jeff and Jill Williams in their landmark book, *Marriage Coaching: Heart, Hope and Skills for a Great Relationship*, have made a very personal deposit in our marriage. Helping us navigate emotional minefields, these tools create a safe place for us to express our feelings and know that we are heard; to share and hold one another's hearts. When our typical conversations fail, we lean into the skills Jeff and Jill taught us and find that our relational landmines are defused and resolved. Our path to growth is accelerated and protected when we embrace this healthy process.

Jerome & Kellie Daley
Co-authors, *Not Your Parents Marriage*. www.purposecoach.net

---

In a day and age in which marriages are breaking down in record numbers the Williams' offer hope. Marriages can be restored. Husbands and wives can experience rich, healthy relationships and greater intimacy within their lives together. Further, out of the ashes of hurt and pain can rise up Marriage Coaching couples who represent Christ, His love to the world, and a heart for reconciliation. The principles contained within this book flow from lives that have walked the road, experienced deep pain, paid the price, and co-operated with God to see relationship restored. The authentic journey the Williams' freely share will capture your heart, while inspiring and teaching you how to effectively hold the heart of your spouse (and become a model of healthy relationship for others). Indeed, there is hope for marriages today.

Gregory Bland
Lead Pastor, Coach, and author of *Pro-Active Parent Coaching: Capturing the Heart of Your Child*, www.proactivefamilies.com

---

Jeff is my friend. I have watched him lead with the unique gift of boldness mixed with compassion. He has mediated both personal and professional relationships for me with great effectiveness. The gift he and Jill have to help bring life to marriages is truly from Father. Their insight and wisdom into the process of healing relationships is changing lives in my community. *Marriage Coaching: Heart, Hope and Skills for a Great Relationship* is more than a lesson plan of good techniques, it's real life instruction for transformation!

Rob Rue
C.F.S.P. (Certified Funeral Service Practitioner)
Vice President & Co-Owner of Littleton & Rue Funeral Home & Crematory. Founder of LiveNow - Promoting an Active Lifestyle (ilivenow.org)

At a time when our marriage needed a boost, my husband and I discovered Jeff and Jill Williams' Marriage Coaching Teleclass. We were amazed by how quickly our communication improved as we simply practiced the straightforward steps Jeff and Jill taught us. Now we're delighted to see these same tools become available to couples around the world. Thank you, Jeff and Jill, for doing the hard work in your own marriage that has allowed you to discover God's timeless truths, then develop them into easy-to-use principles that—once applied—build the kind of intimacy couples long for with the one they love most in this world.

Dr. Myra Perrine
LIFE Coach, Church Resource Ministries
Adjunct professor, Simpson University & Tozer Theological Seminary. Author: *What's Your God Language?*, *Touching the Hem of His Garment, Hearing the Voice of the Shepherd,* and *Passionate Spirituality: Preparing for the Bridegroom.*

Jeff and Jill share their overwhelming passion for abundant, life-giving marriages by teaching coaching tools that couples can use to help their own marriages grow and prosper. There are many examples from their own marriage and many scenarios of couples they have worked with, that will give couples much hope right from the get-go that their relationships can be what they always dreamed of them being. Marriage Coaching was part of what helped us to reconcile our marriage so we're confident that it might help you (see our reconciliation story in chapter 11).

Richard & Sharon Wildman
Stubborn Pursuits Ministries, www.stubbornpursuits.wordpress.com.

Jeff and Jill have given birth to a "child" they have been carrying their whole lives, especially during the several decades of their own marriage. Personal interactions with them the past six years have demonstrated to us how deeply committed they are to healthy marriages, including their own. They share and facilitate out of their own struggles and victories, recounting with great transparency the "birth pangs" that are now resulting in this useful resource for motivated couples.

A key difference between this book and many others on marriage is that it is not just self-help. Couples are definitely equipped with tools and skills for their own marriage. However, the over-arching vision Jeff and Jill communicate is that it doesn't stop there. It goes beyond adding to multiplying. Chapter 11 on "A Marriage Built for Others" turns a crucial corner with the opening sentences:

When God initiates healing and growth it isn't just for us, but also for others. His purpose in blessing us is that we might be a blessing. What you receive from God for your marriage is for you AND for others: your children, their children, your family, friends, and the Church.

Our prayers for this book is that its influence and positive impact become transformational catalysts in the same way that God's promise to Abraham carried blessing beyond his own household and generation. Thank you, Jeff and Jill, for your labor of love!

Lavern & Ronda Nissley
Directors of Marriage Resource Center of Miami Valley
www.marriageresourcecenter.org
Authors: *RINGS (Real Intimacy and Growth Skills) Workbook* and *RINGS Marriage Mentoring Companion Guide*

Your marriage can get the excitement back! We have used the skills in this book for several years, and we can tell you, from determined experience, that being intentional about learning and practicing a new way to listen and ask questions will take your relationship to a more enjoyable and pleasurable place. And - it will be richer and fuller because of what you experience together.

Porter & Joanie Shellhammer
Relationship Coaches
Sarasota, FL

Jeff and Jill are pioneers in developing the new and exciting methodology of Marriage Coaching. I'm excited because it breaks new ground in relating solid principles, demonstrated through stories and examples both from their experience of coaching others and from their own marriage. Practical, clear and easy to read, this excellent book provides a road map of the process needed for marital transformation.

Tina Stoltzfus Horst
Founder and Executive Director, Coaching Mission International, www.coachingmission.com

---

If you're willing to work and fight for your marriage, then there is hope and healing in these pages. With Spirit and heart Jeff and Jill Williams provide the tools that can transform your relationship. I've seen the results firsthand. Coaching Your Own Marriage can help take you from the battlefield back into the bedroom.

Wayne Herninko
Licensed Teacher
Certified Leadership Coach

Table of Contents

Acknowledgements

The authors of this book *should be* the group of people from whom we have learned so much about great relationships. In recent years you have not only cheered us on but have also been the ones who have graciously taught us how to live what we've written. So many deserve mention by name such as our Friday morning prayer group, home fellowship group and our parents. Their fingerprints are all over this work, and some of them have written endorsements. Thank you. We love all of you!

A couple of people have coached, counseled and befriended us in extraordinary ways that must be mentioned, if only to inspire you to extraordinarily befriend others as they have done. Tony Stoltzfus,[1] you have brilliantly and genuinely articulated Christian Coaching as the discipline of believing in people. The privilege of your friendship means that we have had firsthand experience to verify that you mean what you say and that you live your values with integrity. Thank you. If anyone benefits from what is written in the following pages they owe much to you. You have consistently encouraged, served and believed in what could be. There is no way this would have come to fruition and that we would be living our calling if you had not dared to believe that coaching could help marriages and that God wanted to use us to inspire and equip others to do it too. Saying thank you isn't enough, yet we know your reward is to continue to see this paid forward into the lives of others.

Richard and Sharon Wildman are a very special couple who have blessed us in unreasonable ways including steadfast friendship for many years. You remained by our side to speak hope and belief into us and our calling, and you have generously given oodles of practical support. I fondly remember the winter day we sat in a coffee shop and you made crystal clear in a loving confrontation why this writing must be done;

for other couples that are as desperate as you once were. Thank you for your faithfulness and thank you for laboring now to tell your story of reconciliation that is certain to help countless other couples.[2]

Thank you to our counseling clients dating back to 1988 and the numerous couples that we taught Marriage Coaching in private sessions, seminars and classes. Some of you have been through more beta versions of our trials and errors than you deserve, and you have been more gracious in your critiques than we deserve. It is wonderful that you have not only found help for yourselves, but also that you are now passing it on to others.

From Jeff to Jill: Darling, our marriage has been a magnificent, grueling, surprising and miraculous, joyful and challenging adventure since the night I tearfully trembled at the altar. As you say, we've grown up together. No man could want for a better, more loyal, loving, committed and wise wife. Anything I know about marriage and how to form and maintain healthy relationships I have either learned from you or with you. The tears on my cheeks as I write are about gratitude for the fact that we are realizing our youthful dream to enjoy a long and abundantly pleasurable and purposeful marriage and that we have survived serious threats to our relationship. I love that we continue the adventure together. I love you.

From Jill to Jeff: I don't think either one of us could have dreamed where we've been in our marriage. It's been amazing and fun, but it's also been so very hard. We have been able to do and see things, people and places that I just never expected. The world has become a whole lot smaller and comfortable to us. I love that most of all; that we could go or do just about anything God called us to do now because of the preparation. When things became really hard I'm glad that we never let "us" deteriorate or considered one another the "problem." It has been a privilege to learn from you, to minister with you and to be stretched as a "team of two." I can't wait to see where/how the journey leads us next. I love you.

Foreword

There are plenty of good books out there on marriage. What makes this one great is that it incorporates some simple, biblical change principles that seem to have been lost for a long time.

Here's a quick way to grasp one of these principles. Ponder this question for a moment: How many ways can you think of that you could be a better husband or wife?

I don't know about you, but my number would be pretty big! My wife's love language is acts of service, and that is not my strength. I could bring her flowers more often, clean up after myself, and take on a few of her responsibilities, set aside more time just to talk... Sort of discouraging to think of all the ways you fall short, isn't it?

Now, let's look at things a little differently. How many things are you really motivated to do for your spouse that you aren't doing? That's a much smaller number! Here's the lesson: knowing what to do does not produce change (otherwise that big list would be much shorter). *Motivation is a far greater predictor of change than information.*

If you are tempted at this point to say, "Duh!" and close the book, hang with me for a minute, because this is profound. In the last church service you attended, how much of the time was spent instructing you on what to do, versus asking what motivates you? In most churches, the ratio is 90 to 100% instruction and very little personal support, practice or interaction. Or if someone came to you for help with their marriage, would your impulse be to offer information and advice, or help them figure it out on their own? The vast majority of us would choose to teach or instruct. If we summarized what we believe about change based solely on our actions, it would be this: *if people know what to do, they will automatically do it.*

Sounds a little off, doesn't it? Yet we operate out of that belief every day. It's funny how we can believe things that seem totally ridiculous once we say them out loud. However, change does not begin with information, or even with discipline: *it starts with desire.*

Coaching is a new way to work at change that is designed around motivation, not instruction. Coaching starts with what *you* want to change based on what God is doing in you, and the whole process is arranged to maximize your motivation—because if you are really motivated, you will really change.

Here are a few more reasons why I believe marriage coaching is becoming an essential tool for revitalizing marriages and growing great relationships:

1. **It appeals to men.**

    The counseling approach is that something is broken or un-healthy that needs help to be fixed. That is a valid approach, but men tend to react negatively to anything that implies they are needy or have failed. Coaching, by contrast, works with people who see themselves as basically healthy and helps them toward a desired future. It's much easier to get a man into marriage coaching than marriage counseling.

2. **It makes people responsible.**

    In coaching you set the agenda, you set the goals and you decide on steps of action. When you choose what to do, your buy-in is higher, and you take more responsibility to get it done.

3. **Coaching focuses on growth.**

    The coaching approach works with healthy marriages as well as strained ones, because it trains couples to meet God in their situation and move forward. Instead of getting healed, couples focus on developing the patterns that produce long-term health and growth.

Jeff and Jill explain in depth exactly how coaching works in this book. They've done a great job of applying the fundamentals of a biblical coaching approach to marriages in a practical, applicable way.

I've walked with Jeff for many years, and I have a deep admiration for his intimacy with God, his generosity, his passion for relationships, and the sacrifices he has made to become a man who could write this book. He has been my personal peer coach for the last few years, and through meeting together every few weeks I've been privileged to share the journey of writing it with him (as well as periodically shoving him from behind to get it done!)

Jeff has combined the best of his background in counseling and therapy with the best of the coaching method to produce a book I believe will be a seminal work in this field. As the Message puts it:

"He said, "Then you see how every student well-trained in God's kingdom is like the owner of a general store who can put his hands on anything you need, old or new, exactly when you need it" (Mt. 13:52).

Tony Stoltzfus
Master coach, author and coach trainer

Introduction

In a sentence, the purpose of this book is to equip you for more and better in your marriage; more hope, pleasure and purpose, and better ways to recover, sustain and to protect it. Learning to coach your marriage is a simple process based on simple skills and exercises so don't be daunted by the idea that it will be difficult to learn. The hope of this fresh self-guided process to heal, strengthen and protect your relationship is that you can know exactly what to do in the most challenging conversations and circumstances with a predictably good outcome.

Despite the statistics that marriage is on the decline and that more than half of today's marriages will eventually fail, it is possible to build and sustain a great marriage! *All it takes to get started is for a couple to agree that they want more and better.*[3] From there it's about heart, hope and skills, which is a formidable combination of humility, desire and ability. While it sounds simple, it isn't easy…but, it's very worthwhile. In the words of my brother in-law before Jill and I married, *"Jeff, it's the hardest thing you'll ever do, and the most worthwhile thing."* He was right.

About the Book

The scope of this book is simultaneously narrow and broad. It is narrow because it presents a few simple foundational concepts and skills for a process that any couple can use to better understand each other's thoughts, feelings and desires, to set goals and to support each other as you pursue those goals for relationship growth or change. *In a nutshell that is the process of coaching your own marriage; a self-guided process that results in the discovery of goals shared by both partners followed by self-monitoring to do the action steps to achieve those goals.*

The scope of this book is also broad because the skills are useful with any marital content at any point in a couple's life cycle, and it is a useful process to help couples consider and apply ideas from other marriage curricula.

Listening, asking, setting goals and supporting the growth and change process with encouragement and accountability are effective skills with many applications. What you will experience as unique in this presentation is the emphasis on heart as the motivator and guide for use of the skills.[4] You'll be challenged to prepare and sustain a hopeful, humble and compassionate heart as the foundation of life-giving conversations facilitated by skills.

About Your Marriage

This book might be the starting point of your marriage journey, an oasis of rejuvenation along the way, or your last purchase while you're trying to decide whether or not to call it quits. Whichever the reason(s) it is in your hands, we want you to know that it has been prayed over in faith. We wholeheartedly believe that if you are willing to receive a miracle from God that He will use something in the pages that follow to give your marriage what He wants for it to make it what He wants it to be.

The vision that compels us to write, coach, and teach is a vision that we invite you to embrace and to become a part of: *Every Christian Marriage experiencing abundant hope, pleasure and purpose for the Kingdom of God.* That is what has sustained our motivation to do the hard work of writing; *so that you can live out your destiny for God's purposes for your marriage AND so that you can enjoy abundant pleasure and joy while you do!*[5]

Getting Started

The following pages will give you practical skills and effective exercises to build and sustain great relationships along with essential concepts to help you understand the principles behind the skills. Every chapter will give you something you can begin doing or do more effectively in your relationships.

Reflection and practice will help you to get the most out of this book. The more you think about how to integrate these skills, process and attitudes into your life, and the more you do them, the more natural it will feel to you. Learning to coach your marriage is one endeavor where the benefits you experience will be proportional to the time and effort you put into it. *Reflection Questions* are at the end of every chapter. We included these to help you get as much as possible from reading by prompting you to verbalize (or journal) insights and desires. Since the discipline of reflection (thinking about our life experiences) is the birthplace of understanding and awareness of desires, it is the first step in setting goals that you and your marriage want to accomplish. Our suggestion about how to use these is to at least privately reflect and pray over them. Next, you may want to discuss your answers with your spouse. Perhaps some shared goals will emerge from your conversation! Finally, it is possible to read the book as a small group or as a team of marriage coaching couples as you build the marriage ministry of your church or community marriage initiative. In addition, there are some other resources and links at the back of the book under the heading, "If you want more."

While Jeff was the primary writer of this book, everything that follows is based on shared personal experience in our marriage, and professionally in our shared ministry of coaching and training couples in Marriage Coaching. It is accurate to assume that we share the same perspective as a team of two and that we could speak interchangeably even when it sounds like Jeff is the primary author speaking in first person.

Enjoy the journey! We'll be praying for you!
Jeff and Jill

PART I

A Fresh Approach to Building
(and sustaining)
a Great Relationship

Ninety Minutes to a Better Marriage

"Perseverance wins the race"
(Aesop; from *The Tortoise and The Hare*)
"Let *us* **not** *become weary in doing good, for at the proper time we will reap a harvest if we do* **not give** *up."* (Galatians 6:9)

A few weeks prior to moving our family from Ohio to Maryland in 2005, I agreed to see a couple for one ninety-minute counseling session. Knowing my time in the area was short, my best judgment said to refer the couple to a colleague who could meet with them as many times as necessary to resolve their issues. I only had time in my schedule to see them once, but they didn't want to be referred. My expectations of what could be accomplished in just one session were low, but I was willing to give it my best. They consented to the one session, paid their fee, and proceeded to tell me their story.

> *"We've been married about 20 years. We are people of faith, who have never considered divorce as an option. We even envisioned helping other couples as a ministry at some point, but that's all changed. A few years ago we adopted a girl who seemed normal, but later we discovered she had attachment disorder. That translates to a lot of conflict and stress with her, and between us. Somehow, she has effectively pitted us against each other in such a bad way that now we are seriously considering divorce. In fact, that's why we insisted on seeing you. We saw another counselor who said that we should separate immediately and file papers for divorce because they didn't see our situation ever getting better.[7] We want a second opinion."*

1

Talk about having a gun to your head! How could I help them in ninety minutes? After a few more questions about their current circumstance I asked one of the most important questions that a people-helper can ask, *"What do you want?"*

> *"We want to stay together. We want better ways to communicate and deal with our conflict. We don't want to separate. We want to restore what's been lost, and maybe even somehow, someday realize our dream of having a marriage good enough that we can inspire and help other couples that get to a desperate place like this. Do you think that's possible?"*
>
> *"Well,"* I replied, *"I definitely think that this is a God-sized dream, and it's going to take some work, but yes, I think it is possible. The great thing is that you both want more and better for your marriage, and that you have a glimmer of hope that it is possible. The bad thing is that you obviously don't yet have the tools that you need to do the job. But that is something we can begin to correct immediately. Let's take the rest of the session for me to teach you some of these, and see how far they get you."*

Over the next hour and a half I learned a lot about what is effective for couples that want to improve their marriage. As I began, I took a deep breath, said a silent prayer and summoned my courage. With no time to waste, I quickly shared what I knew to be the best of the best, hoping that it might get them started, but at the same time believing it would probably not be sufficient. It wasn't enough time.

I taught the couple a few simple exercises to develop skills they could use to ask about and listen to each other's honest thoughts, feelings and desires. What I didn't know then was that that impromptu teaching would become a full-fledged system for helping multitudes of couples to help themselves and to help others.[8] What I taught this desperate couple was to become the core of this book; the heart and skill of *loving listening, curious asking, effective goal-setting and key principles for supporting growth and change.*

This couple was highly motivated. They executed the exercises with sincerity and precision, took notes and asked questions. When our allotted time was finished I took another deep breath, prayed for them, wished them well, provided names and numbers for a few local colleagues who could meet with them in the future, and welcomed them to contact me by phone if they had any questions about how to use the skills or do the exercises.

Two weeks later they called. I held my breath as I answered, *"This is Jeff."*

It was the husband, *"We just wanted to share how helpful we've found what you gave us a couple of weeks ago. We've been able to talk about some hard things and really hear each other. We've negotiated some solutions to parenting issues that had been stuck for a while, and ... we've even been able to be intimate again (It had been six months)."*

I was stunned. *"How in the world did you accomplish all of that?"* I asked.

He continued excitedly, *"It's just like you said. These tools work if you work them with good-will toward the relationship.⁹ We didn't have any other options so we've both given our best to the process you recommended and it's been working. We've not been able to talk like this for a long time. We're not completely out of the woods, but we're definitely on our way. You've got to know that this process works. If there's more where you got it from, we want it."*

Wow! This was definitely an exceptional situation...or was it?

For years Jill and I had prayed for more effective ways to help couples. On an informal basis couples from church had sought us to help them, and more often I counseled couples in my role as a counselor, but I didn't feel very successful in marriage therapy. My conclusion was that either I wasn't trained properly to help them or that the state of the art wasn't that good. Or maybe it was because couples came seeking help so late in the process, after there was a lot of turbulent water already under the bridge. At any rate, the norm for us with marriage counseling was hitting a wall. Our failures as counselors and my personal passion—fueled from being a child of divorce—to sustain a healthy and pleasurable marriage spurred my search, and prayers for wisdom and a better way to work with married couples.

Looking back at my failures, I recognize that I didn't know what I didn't know. But I know now! In fact, Jill and I both know because we've learned it together and that's why we're sharing it with you. Here's the well-kept secret:

> *The state of the art in relationship skills is much better than most couples are aware of. There are proven skills and exercises that can help any couple who wants to grow or change, to prevent misunderstandings, to build closeness, to resolve conflict in a way that builds rather than hurts the relationship, to develop emotional literacy (the ability to identify and express feelings), to build and sustain healthy and pleasurable intimacy, and so much more!*[10]
>
> *And, specifically, the coaching approach is a robust skill-based process to help couples envision the ideal future of their relationship and to make their dreams a reality by setting goals and executing action-steps they develop and choose!*

We would never claim that this book is the only book you need to build and sustain a great marriage. The fact is that there are a plethora of models and approaches that our colleagues have developed. But we are confident about the effectiveness of this approach, because of the foundational principles and tools it presents, and because it has worked in our marriage, and hundreds of others.[11]

The fact is that the story about the couple in this chapter is not an uncommon story for couples who avail themselves of state of the art concepts and skills to apply to their relationship. And since this approach worked for a couple in an extremely challenging and painful situation, maybe it will work for you.

What do YOU want?

What do you want for your marriage? Why did you pick up this book? Do you want more and better for your marriage? We do. Why? Because our marriage has been to hell and back; we didn't like hell and we don't want to go back. We never expected things to take a turn for the worse in our relationship. It isn't what we thought about on our wedding day. No one does. But our story is a common story.

When Jill and I fell in love, we decided we would be happier together than apart, so we tied the knot. We were young, and we were dumb. Well, at the very least we were ignorant about what it would take to build and sustain a pleasurable and purposeful marriage. We were what you would call "unconsciously incompetent," or in laymen terms: we didn't know what we didn't know.[12] But, both providence and necessity have combined to equip us with helpful knowledge and experience. As Jill says, *"We've grown up together."*

Two kids, who at ages 20 and 21 naively tied the knot 25 years ago, are now in their mid-forties with plenty of battle scars to prove that we've failed our way forward, persisting on the journey that began with love and continued with stubbornness. We refused to be a statistic of divorce and always wanted more than a mediocre marriage.

While we've enjoyed a lot of pleasure, we've also had pain. Often it has been self-inflicted, and many times we've stayed in painful places longer than necessary. Had we known how to coach ourselves earlier in our marriage I think we would have been more efficient at resolving pain and sustaining pleasure. We hope that this book catches some of you near the start of your marriage so that you can navigate your journey better equipped than we were.

At one point in our marriage, life conspired to put us in a pit for a season. During that time we learned how to get out of the pit and how to avoid going there again. Perhaps you are not in the pit, but are looking for a way to maximize the potential of your marriage. Maybe it's good, but you think it could be better. Or maybe it's not so great: there is some pain from the past nagging at you that you don't know how to talk about, or ongoing conflict. Perhaps some of your needs aren't being met. Or, perhaps you are one of the rare couples that are simply motivated to proactively protect your marriage.

Maybe you've tried counseling or marriage seminars and you're burned out. They were good, as far as they went, but you want something fresh, and you want something you can use right away that will make a difference. The reality for some couples is that they can't find anyone willing or competent to help. If that's your circumstance, then we hope this book will begin to provide some hope and practical help for at least part of your journey.

From the experience of Jill and me, it is clear that marriage can be heaven or it can be hell, and sometimes it changes on a moment's notice! As they say about the weather in some places, *If you don't like it, wait an hour. It will change.* Couples in marriages of any length probably agree that at the minimum, marriage can be bland, monotonous and boring. At its worst it is very painful. But it *can be* very fulfilling, exciting and meaningful. How is it for you? Where are you in your marriage? And what do you want? The concepts and skills in this book have helped us to make our good marriage better, but it has also helped us through horrid periods of crisis and pain. Regardless of where you find yourselves in marriage, this can help you do the same in your marriage.

But it's Too Late, We Are out of Time!

Can you identify with our story, or at least parts of it? Whatever your reasons are for picking up this book, our promise to you is to get down to the nitty-gritty of the essential ingredients that Jill and I have personally used to save, strengthen and protect our own marriage, and to help hundreds of other couples to build and sustain abundant marriages for themselves and others.

Some of you might be thinking it's too late; that too much water has passed under the bridge and that somehow parts, or the whole, of your marriage are irrecoverable. To that we say, "Phooey!" Today is the first day of the rest of your marriage. As you learn to coach your own marriage you might join the ranks of others who have been very pleasantly surprised to find themselves capable and willing to revisit and bring closure to past challenging issues and build new communication skills.

If your marriage is at a crisis point, you may want to flip to the bonus chapter on crisis management at the end of the book for some specialized encouragement for marriages in crisis. But don't miss the rest of the book. If you only read the chapter on crisis, you won't have all of the essential ingredients you need to coach your marriage through a healing process.

Whatever is happening in your marriage, it's not too late, and you are not out of time—but you will need to invest some time going forward. Any couple that has ever sought help for their marriage, even for a simple refresher or tune-up weekend has faced some harsh realities about the limitations of the event, their mentors, counselors or coaches; *they didn't go home with them.*[13] The best and most attentive and involved marriage therapists, coaches, mentors and pastors only spend a fraction of life with a couple. On average, it's 1/168th of a week; only one of the 168 hours in a week. At best, couples who attend marriage intensives get 30 hours/week for two weeks from therapists, but still they too eventually have to leave the safety net of the retreat, or the "neutral ground" of an appointment with those that are helping them to communicate better.

We tell our clients that even if we meet with them on a regular basis for the rest of their marriage that we will not be able to cover all of the content that encompasses their relationship. There are so many nuanced thoughts, feelings and desires that couples experience in their day-to-day life that it is impossible to cover even a small part of them in the span of an hour or 90 minute weekly session.

So, where's the hope in a little book? And, what's the 90 minute promise that the title of this chapter inferred? *The hope is in the process, and the great thing is that once you learn it, it can be used with any content.* What do we mean? Check out a conversation we had with some clients recently.

"Before we get started we need to be clear about what we mean about the difference between process and content. Because

we are aiming to work ourselves out of a job by giving you a lot of help as quickly as possible, we are going to intentionally focus more on the process of your communication, conflict resolution, and handling of emotionally charged issues than the actual content. It's not that we aren't interested or don't care about the content, but the reality is that we will never be able to hear all the content of your relationship in the time that we spend together in Marriage Coaching sessions. But you can, and you will have to on your own time if you are going to get and keep a great marriage."

"What's realistic is for you to expect to learn a process you can use to communicate about all of the unique content issues of your marriage (e.g., finances, schedule, intimacy, children) in a way that strengthens the bond between you by using skills and exercises designed to get to the heart of your heart in a way that respects and protects your relationship. Does this make sense?"

"Many couples come to us with the assumption that we need to hear all of their issues in detail before we will be able to help them. We don't. We simply need to understand the basic improvements that a couple would like to make in order to decide where to begin teaching concepts and modeling skills and exercises for them to use at home."

"When you have a process in hand to successfully negotiate the content of your relationship, you can continue to use that process to address other challenges you face in the future. Of course there might be specific information helpful in such situations, for instance, if one of you were to experience chronic illness, or financial difficulties, empty nest syndrome, etc., but still, the process to communicate your honest thoughts and feelings with each other, to resolve conflict, to handle strong emotions, to set and work on relationship goals remains constant, regardless of the new content."

"Let us illustrate. In the U.S.A., baseball is the national pastime. Every major league game is played by the same

process; nine innings, home team bats last, three outs per inning, and if the game is tied at the end of nine innings, extra innings are played until one team is ahead at the end of an inning. But, the content of every major league game is different. The players, team names, duration of games, and the cities in which they are played are all different. The content of every game is different, but the process is the same."

It's not too late for your marriage, if you'll invest a few hours in reading AND using the skills and exercises outlined in this book you will be well on your way to effectively coaching your own marriage and will be pleasantly surprised at the results!

CHAPTER ONE
Reflection Questions:

1. How did you decide to read, *Marriage Coaching: Heart, Hope and Skills for a Great Relationship*?

_____

_____

_____

_____

_____

2. What do you want to get from this book? What outcome from reading it would let you say that it was worth your time to read it?

_____

_____

_____

_____

_____

3. How did the lead story about the 90-minute session impact you?

_____

_____

_____

_____

_____

What is Marriage Coaching?

Before we share the skills you need to coach your own marriage, we need to explain what Marriage Coaching is and how we use it to help couples to heal, and strengthen and protect their marriage. This will help you to begin to understand how to apply coaching to your marriage.

Christian Marriage Coaching is the application of Christian coaching concepts and skills to facilitate growth and change for couples.[14] Below is a brief introduction to Christian coaching. Everything that applies to coaching individuals applies to coaching couples.[15]

> *One, Christian coaching is fundamentally client-centered and directed.* The client is the focus: their needs, the issues they want to work on and helping them discover what they are motivated to change.
>
> *Two, the Christian coaching relationship is essentially transparent and authentic.* The coach models relational authenticity including transparency to the person(s) being coached with the desire that the client will be able to do the same in the relationship.
>
> *Three, Christian coaching is empowering.* As the coach empowers the client to work on the issues that are most important to them, the client is helped to focus on the development of goals and the action steps necessary to achieve those goals.

For those who have successfully utilized coaching concepts, it has proven to be an effective, efficient and comprehensive way to move a person toward change. And the process is completely transferable: it can be used in multiple relationships and different circumstances.

In general, individual coaching is an empowering voluntary authentic relationship in which coach and client focus on clarifying goals that the client wants to accomplish.

Instead of focusing on the individual, the objective of Marriage Coaching is to facilitate identification of growth goals that both partners are motivated to pursue. Once goals are determined, the coaching couple collaborates with the couple being coached to develop and choose action steps to accomplish those goals. *Couples that coach their own marriage practice the discipline of believing in themselves and their marriage by actively pursuing growth and change through a process in which they keep themselves responsible.*

This process is obviously more challenging than coaching individuals because each partner's perspective must be drawn out, clarified and understood before goals are negotiated and decided, and action steps are chosen.

While Marriage Coaching is offered as a service by trained couples (from lay to professional), its reliance on basic skills such as asking, listening, and setting goals makes it an approach that any couple can quickly learn to use to help their own marriage. Couples can learn skills and a process in a relatively brief period of time—when compared to the amount of time spent in an average counseling relationship—and then begin to apply them at home.[16]

Let's look at a couple different scenarios. The first is about a couple experiencing a significant crisis due to an inappropriate relationship, a situation that facilitated the birth of Marriage Coaching. The second is about a marriage facing a more ordinary circumstance. Follow the process used in both situations to help you understand what Marriage Coaching is and how it works.

The Birth of Marriage Coaching—Two Couples in Crisis

"Jeff, I've got a bad situation here. Two marriages are in crisis because of an inappropriate relationship. We know you have extensive experience in situations like this. Will you and Jill come to help?"

The two couples were in pain and undecided about their futures. The extensive involvement of both families in a church meant that there could be catastrophic ramifications not only for them, but the entire congregation. Why? People talk and take sides. It's not uncommon for such events to erode unity or even split churches. The best outcome in such a circumstance would be reconciled relationships in both marriages and between the couples.

With a tone that communicated pastoral concern mixed with a tinge of desperation, the pastor asked me to get on the next available flight to his city: *"We'll pay your expenses and have you here as long as it takes; whatever you need."*

Providentially, our schedule was open. *"We'll be glad to come,"* I said. As soon as I hung up the phone, adrenaline rushed through my body as I began to contemplate how Jill and I could help these two couples. I caught the first plane with an empty seat the next morning and Jill followed a couple days later.

En route I contemplated: *What had we learned and experienced over the years that we could apply to this broken situation?* A few years prior we helped to catalyze a community marriage initiative,[17] in the process learning the state of the art in relationship ministry. The big secret was the existence of relationship skills that almost any couple could learn to use to improve communication, prevent misunderstandings, build closeness and resolve conflicts in ways that build instead of eroding their relationship.

Just prior to the community marriage initiative I'd become certified as a Christian Leadership Coach.[18] As I reflected on the community initiative and coach training I thought, *We'll draw on the most effective relationship concepts and skills we know to help them work through pain while we're with them, and to equip them with coaching skills to continue dealing with hard issues effectively after we're gone.* When I compared notes with Jill over the phone that evening I discovered that she'd reached the same conclusion. So, as we flew into the storm of the relationship crisis, Marriage Coaching was born.[19]

Arriving on the scene, we formatted our conversations with both couples, and the church leaders as a coaching conversation. We worked through a coaching process called "The Coaching Funnel". The concept of the funnel is to help a client discover their vision for what an ideal future looks like, progressing through an exploration of their thoughts, feelings and desires. You then assist the client to set clear, specific and measurable goals, to move them toward their ideal future, with

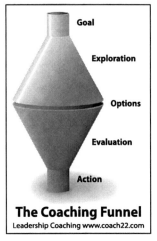

The Coaching Funnel
Leadership Coaching www.coach22.com

action steps to achieve those goals. After working through the coaching funnel, we taught and modeled communication and conflict resolution exercises based on the skills in this book. Sounds easy, right?

In many respects it was easy. Although the situation was emotionally charged and extremely uncomfortable, we knew exactly how to structure every session in order to obtain clear objectives based on what the participants wanted. They wanted to understand what happened and why it happened, so we facilitated partners sharing with each other using good speaking and listening skills. Some wanted apologies and others wanted forgiveness, so we facilitated them through apologies. They wanted ways to work through the powerful emotions they were carrying, so we modeled exercises to help them to do just that.

The process elicited their desires and we simply responded to what they asked for. That's the foundation of coaching; it's about what the person/relationship being coached wants, not what someone else — counselor, pastor, friend — prescribes for them. So, coaching your own marriage is about the desires of your heart, and that's why it works. You and your spouse identify what you want, and then work a process to make your desires reality!

Now let's listen in on the Marriage Coaching session of a couple facing more ordinary circumstances. Hear the flow of the conversation, and then we'll anticipate some of your questions about Marriage Coaching.

An Average Couple in Marriage Coaching

Bob and Patrice said their marriage was stagnant. They didn't have huge issues, but most couples don't seek help unless something is painful.

> "We have a few sticking points and want to be proactive to solve them instead of waiting for things to get worse. That's what we've heard from couples that eventually got divorced; that they had some minor problems that grew into bigger problems that eventually destroyed them." Said Patrice, "We want to head off any problems before they grow bigger."

Both Bob and Patrice noticed some negative patterns in their relationship they wanted to break, and they were both agreeable to setting some goals to see the needed change happen. The crux of the issues was that their communication became strained during Bob's busy season at work; times that Patrice didn't feel Bob heard her concerns or cared about her. Patrice's sense of alienation resulted in her being less than willing to be sexually intimate with Bob—a problem for him, as it would be for most men. Bob agreed that communication could be improved on his part, and yes, he wanted more physical intimacy.

> "We're not sure that things are so complicated that we need counseling," Bob stated, "But we do feel stuck and want some help. The coaching approach sounds interesting. What is it?"
>
> I replied, "Basically, Marriage Coaching is a conversation about how you want to grow and change in your marriage. As a Marriage Coaching couple, Jill and I will ask questions to understand what you want to be different in your relationship, and to help the two of you to choose one or more goals. You set the goals and choose the steps to achieve the goals. We facilitate your conversations, and provide support, encouragement and accountability to accomplish the goals you set. We'll

be happy to share ideas about how to accomplish your goals from strategies we've used and that we've seen other couples use, but only after you've maxed out your own creative ideas, and only if you want to hear some ideas to consider. The coaching approach is about building your capacity to solve your own problems, and your confidence to do that will grow if you push yourselves and allow us to push you through the process of creative brain-storming."

Finishing my explanation, I asked, "How does that sound?"

"It sounds great to me," Bob said. "I've used a process like that at work, and it's been really effective."

We met with Bob and Patrice four times for sessions of about 90 minutes over three months. They quickly set two goals in our first session, practiced some skills and exercises in our second session, ironed out some kinks in the process in the third session, and celebrated what they'd accomplished in the fourth. That's when they said they had what they needed, and were ready to stop meeting. We were amazed by how quickly they understood and applied what we taught them, but that is often the case.

Coaching skills and process is so easily understood, embraced and put to use by couples that we are no longer surprised by quick progress. Now, like many other clients, they are coaching their own marriage by using the skills they learned. That doesn't mean they won't ever seek or need to seek assistance from a Marriage Coaching couple again. They might get stuck if a new issue arises. But unless and until that happens, they know exactly how to help themselves by coaching their own marriage.

Bob and Patrice remain one of our best sources of referrals. Sometimes they informally teach other couples what they learned from us, but when a situation seems beyond their comfort level, they refer to us. They could do more coaching of other couples if they went through a lay Christian Marriage Coaching training process, but it's not the right season of life for them to do that yet. At least for now they have a good taste in their mouth for the process and are strong advocates of the process.

Now for some of the questions that may have come to your mind while reading the two coaching scenarios:

One: How is Marriage Coaching different from counseling or mentoring?

As a Marriage Coaching couple we are apt to hear about pain and emotions from the couples we coach—like in the first scenario with the marriage infidelity—but we don't behave as counselors who diagnose the problems and prescribe solutions. Instead we focus on facilitating couples to have life-giving conversations with skills that they can use themselves outside of coaching sessions to develop their own solutions to the issues they consider important.

Different than marriage counseling, Marriage Coaching relies on a client couple's expertise and familiarity with their desires for their relationship instead of the counselor's specialized knowledge. And goals that a couple sets for their marriage are personal goals, never goals that the marriage coaches set for them. Remember, we helped the couples in the first scenario through apologies, forgiveness and an understanding of what exactly happened—all desires of the two couples being coached.

Unlike its differences with marriage counseling, Marriage Coaching and marriage mentoring do share some similarities. Both coaches and mentors are free to share information from their personal relationship or ministry experience during sessions, but unlike mentor couples, Marriage Coaching couples share only when the couple that is being coached asks or gives permission to do so.

When they do share ideas, Marriage Coaching couples are careful not to prescribe or require couples being coached to choose specific goals or action steps. It is always the client couple's choice about how to apply what they learn from their coaching couple. This is because coaches embrace the value of "Own Life Responsibility"[20] as well as respecting the right and importance of a couple to choose their own goals because they are the ones that have to live with the outcome of their choices. Remember, we told Bob and Patrice that we would be willing to give them some ideas of how they could achieve their goals, but only after they had exhausted their own creativity and ideas.

Asking and listening, and giving the clients choice of goals and action steps are the core of Marriage Coaching that distinguish Marriage Coaching from counseling or mentoring approaches. While counselors and mentors may ask, listen and encourage goal-setting, generally they also take liberty to give unsolicited advice and to require homework or compliance with recommendations as a condition for serving them.[21] In Marriage Coaching, as soon we finish sharing an idea for an action-step we return to a coaching posture to ask the couple being coached, *"What do you think about that? What do you want? Is there anything in those ideas that you would like to consider or to build on as a potential action-step or strategy to accomplish your goal?"*

Two: What is the ultimate objective of Marriage Coaching?

The objective of Marriage Coaching is to facilitate identification of growth goals that both partners are motivated to pursue, and the action steps to accomplish those goals. Once goals are determined marriage coaches help couples to develop action steps.

This process is obviously more challenging than coaching individuals because each partner's perspective must be drawn out, clarified and understood before goals are negotiated and decided, and action steps are chosen. This is one reason that we choose to train couples and not individuals to do Marriage Coaching.[22] Coaching couples as a team of two gives us an opportunity to share the workload of a coaching conversation with a couple. Plus, more territory is covered more quickly, and it is less likely for things to be missed.[23]

Three: What role does the motivation of the couple play in the coaching process?

Marriage Coaching is the discipline of believing in a couple that engages them where God is motivating them to grow or change that keeps them responsible for the process. It is distinct from counseling because Marriage Coaching only attempts to serve couples that want to grow and change, and who are willing to do the process together in order to accomplish something that they both want. In scenario one both couples were motivated to see their marriages healed and restored; in scenario two, Bob and Patrice were motivated to get "unstuck".

In Marriage Coaching, the couple being coached doesn't have to know exactly what changes they want to make when they come to their coaching session. As coaches, we help them to clarify how they want to grow by asking them powerful questions that can draw out their thoughts feelings and desires; and by taking them through exercises that help them communicate what they want to each other.

Four: Can coaching help couples experiencing pain or crisis in their relationship?

Often it is the pain during a crisis that motivates an individual or couple to seek assistance for their marriage. We welcome couples to be coached in such situations because there is nothing like pain to motivate them to focus on what's important.

Our sincere desire to help the two couples in crisis and the church in the first story motivated us to reach for the best of the best in our arsenal. Too much was at stake to use anything other than proven and trustworthy concepts and skills. Two marriages were on life support, and we wanted to do our part to cooperate with God's desire to save them and to protect the church.

The scary thing to us is that if we had been invited to assist a similar situation five years earlier we wouldn't have been as equipped to be helpful. Sadly, that's the situation for many people-helpers and the couples that get help from them; they still don't know what they don't know; *that the state of the art is very good!*

Despite the level of pain or crisis in a relationship, the coaching approach can facilitate healing.[24] We have seen a lot of healing between couples as we simply help them to share their honest thoughts, feelings and desires with each other, while practicing effective listening and respecting and protecting their spouse's heart. Add to that effective asking that opens their hearts to one another to effective goal-setting that helps them to pursue fulfillment of the desires of their heart and a lot can be accomplished for couples, *and by couples for themselves*.[25]

Five: Can the coaching approach deal with the emotions that inevitably go along with the pain?

For some individuals, the mention of emotions or pain in the coaching process can raise a red flag: *I thought coaching was about achieving goals, not dealing with emotions, or things in the past.* We agree that other applications of coaching can be primarily a cognitive process. But we don't see how emotions, pain or the past can be avoided in relationships. Humans aren't just thinking beings. We are also emotional, and few things trigger more emotion than pleasure or disappointment in relationships.

As long as both partners in a marriage are motivated to grow and change, and willing to take responsibility for the process, a coaching approach can at least be a part of the successful formula for a couple to heal, strengthen and protect their marriage, even with the presence of some strong emotions.[26] The coaching sessions with the two couples in the first scenario were full of strong emotions and deep pain. Part of the coaching process was helping the individuals get to the healing that came with apologies and forgiveness.

Six: Do you use a different coaching approach based on the different issues in a marriage?

No. The principles and skills that we used to help the two couples out of a horrible situation are *not just for relationships on the rocks*. It's a set of skills and a process that can be helpful to any couple motivated to grow and change. The nuts and bolts of the skills we used in both scenarios above are the same that we use to coach our own marriage on a daily basis: effective listening, effective asking and effective goal-setting and attainment.

Remember what we asked the couples in the first scenario:
- *What were their honest thoughts, feelings and desires?*
- *Which desires did they want individually and which ones were shared?*
- *What would they be willing to work on together?*

The fact that we began with these questions in an extreme case says something; *that even the most difficult marriage situations can be helped by effective skills for basic communication and understanding.* In fact, we can't think of a relationship situation in which they aren't required.

You may never face what these couples in extreme crisis faced (we hope you don't) but if effective listening that holds the heart of your spouse, asking that opens the heart, and goal-setting that honors the desires of the heart was good for them, then it will likely be helpful to you no matter where you are on a continuum of marriage challenges.

Seven: What is the role of faith in the coaching process?

Jill and I encourage couples to engage the coaching process in faith that they will accomplish what they hope for but don't yet see or experience in their relationship.[27] Most couples that ask for Marriage Coaching are motivated by some degree of pain or lack of pleasure; either something is happening in the marriage that is painful to one of them, or something is missing that would bring more pleasure if it were present.

This makes the faith element of Marriage Coaching essential. Couples that have a history together sometimes have a hard time believing that things can be different; that their partner can act differently. We address this up front by asking the miracle question: *"If God wants to give you a miracle for your marriage, would you be willing to receive it?"* This establishes a baseline of faith to begin the process. From that point on, if ever one or the other says that they won't or can't change, we revisit their original answer: *"But you said that you would receive a miracle from God, and perhaps He is going to do one. Let's continue to pray for that and see what He does."*

Miracle talk can be easy in one respect. *It's like dreaming about what might be. But as the saying goes, dreams are cost-free aspirations, while goals have a budget and a plan. That's why we talk about using the skills and process of Marriage Coaching as the due diligence, our part to steward the miracle that God is going to give a couple in their marriage!*

Eight: How do I know I will get good advice from my coach?

Parameters on Marriage Coaching make it safe for the clients and for the coaches. These include the distinction that marriage coaches are not clinically trained to diagnose problems and prescribe solutions (it's not their job to give you advice), and that all decisions about a relationship belong to the client—the married couple.

Coaches facilitate communication, conflict resolution and goal-setting through asking and listening and facilitating couples to ask and listen to each other. Marriage coaches NEVER tell another couple what to do, but they can share ideas from personal and professional experience in marriage with permission from the couple being coached. Are you getting the picture?

Marriage Coaching, just like individual life and leadership coaching is a client-centered, client-directed process in which the coaches help a couple to explore issues they want to explore and set goals that they choose.

Nine: What do you believe are God's purposes for Marriage Coaching?

Jill and I have been amazed to see how much couples can benefit from a coaching approach to their marriage. *It seems to be an idea whose time has come; couples learning skills to help themselves and other couples to heal, strengthen and protect their marriage.* Why would God reveal and develop this application of coaching at this time?

The importance of a strong and healthy Church[28] in an increasingly tumultuous world is clear. Marriage is the irreducible unit of relationship in the Church that also reflects and models the relationship of Christ the Bridegroom with His Bride, the Church. One couple at a time and one congregation of His Church at a time we see Him moving couples toward a process to heal, strengthen and protect their marriages as part of His move to strengthen the Church. Why? *We think it is because He has purposes to accomplish in the world that will not be carried out until the Church's health and strength is equal to the tasks He wants done.*

The bad news is that the Church has big problems with marriage; the divorce rate among Christians is no different than non-Christians. The good news, however, is that God has given us a way to build, protect and heal marriages.

OK. Hopefully you understand a little more about what Marriage Coaching is. Now it's time to focus on your marriage!

CHAPTER TWO
Reflection Questions:

1. What are the key differences that you see between Marriage Coaching and traditional approaches to helping marriages?

   _____

   _____

   _____

   _____

   _____

2. What excites you about Marriage Coaching for your marriage? What excites you for other couples that you might want to help?

   _____

   _____

   _____

   _____

   _____

3. At this early stage of learning about Marriage Coaching what are your desires? What questions do you have and how do you hope this might be helpful in your marriage?

   _____

   _____

   _____

   _____

   _____

Your Marriage is the Client

Tony and Nikki came to us in crisis. Harsh words had been exchanged between them on more than one occasion. Dysfunctional patterns of communication combined with the pressures of their jobs and raising a family left them with little time and energy for each other. The pleasure of their marriage had eroded and they weren't sure how to get it back. They came to their first session with us feeling pretty bad and unsure how to help their relationship.

Four months and many sessions later they announced that they were going to take a vacation together. Their kids were going too but his family would watch them so Tony and Nikki could enjoy a few days alone. They hoped to use the time alone to rekindle their romance, but problems quickly arose.

Tony and Nikki's vision of a romantic time alone was nearly ruined by a disagreement that became emotionally charged. As our clients for the few months before the trip, they wished that they could see us for a session. But, they were 3000 miles away in a South American hotel. They could have called, but decided instead to try what they had learned over the months. It was only their creative application of skills they'd learned while receiving Marriage Coaching that saved their vacation.

It's a point that all couples who are successfully coached eventually come to; emancipation from those that have taught and encouraged them. Similar to successfully raising children, as coaches we expect and encourage the couples we coach to utilize the principles and skills we taught them on their own, when they're ready—approaching their marriage as a client separate from each of their individual needs and desires.

Pillow Talk

*"Since we couldn't see you we asked ourselves, 'What can we do?'
So, we made name tags, Jeff and Jill, and fastened them on a couple
of the pillows on the bed in our hotel room. We set our chairs in front
of the pillows to make it seem as if we were really with you guys, and
then we started to talk. When we got stuck we turned to the pillows,
and asked, 'What would Jeff and Jill have us do at this point? Guess
what? It worked!'"*

It worked because they'd learned a process to have effective conversations. They'd learned to effectively listen to each other, to ask
effective questions, to set shared goals, and finally, how to support and
encourage each other through the process of working on their goals. To
this day Jill and I have no idea what the content of their hotel conversation was about, and it doesn't matter. They clearly learned enough
from their time with us to effectively coach their own marriage, and
that's what it's all about; *couples using the ingredients they need to
help themselves rather than perpetually depending on others to tell
them what they need to do!*

*Any couple motivated to grow and change in their marriage and
willing to take responsibility for the process can learn to have effective
conversations in which they share honest thoughts, feelings and desires,
develop and pursue shared goals, resolve conflict and negotiate for
changes in the relationship.* Again, it may not be the only approach
they need, and it may not be appropriate if certain issues or dynamics
are present,[29] but for many couples it is enough to take them where
they want to go. This is the power and the promise of the coaching
process: *Once Marriage Coaching is imparted to a couple they will
eventually be able to do for themselves what was done for them.[30]*

Tony and Nikki were stunned when they discovered how much
they'd learned and how well they were able to use the skills we'd shown
them. When faced with a conflict and no easy access to outside help,
they pushed themselves to do well for their marriage by coaching it—
not trying to fix each other or to win an argument. After all, who cares
more for one's marriage; the couple, the coach, counselor, pastor, etc.?

If outside help had been available they might have presented their marriage as a client to be served by someone else. As it was, they asked what their marriage needed and then worked together to brainstorm an option they both liked. Finally, they used a process that they thought would help them to resolve their conflict, and it did!

Tony and Nikki asked themselves how they could respect and protect their relationship and get on with a positive vacation. They opened each other's hearts with effective questions, held each other's hearts with effective listening, and developed a shared goal to resolve their disagreement and to meet each other's needs. Pretty cool, huh? *Again, this is a process that any motivated couple can use effectively as part of their strategy to heal, strengthen and protect their own marriage.*

Your Marriage is Your Client

Married couples are surprised, relieved and inspired when we tell them that their marriage is our client in the Marriage Coaching process. They are surprised because they come expecting a narrow focus on them as individuals. Instead, we elevate the discussion to the level of a partnership and a team which they find easier to talk about. They are relieved because it takes them off the hot seat of individual examination, and because it decreases the potential for the conversation to become adversarial.

Instead, the conversation is about how their behavior affects the entity of the marriage partnership. It is a concept that inspires and motivates couples to give to something bigger than either of them as individuals. *A couple's marriage as the object of their efforts* is an essential concept for a couple to keep at the forefront of their minds as they coach their own marriage. *"What does our marriage need?"* is a more effective question to ask than, *"What do I want?"*

As coaches we make the following pledge to the couples we coach:

"We aren't for either of you individually, but for your marriage. Your union and partnership is above and beyond either of you as individuals. It is a sacred entity unto itself, to

which you both make contributions. Adversarial relationships belong in the legal domain of life, not in marriage. Therefore, we won't side with either of you against the other, but we will encourage both of you to grow and change in ways that will be good for your relationship. If we suggest that one of you start or stop doing something, it will be for the sake of your marriage."

How Our Marriage Ended up in Bed!

Take a step back from your marriage as if you are an objective observer—look at your marriage as the client. **What does your marriage need?** If you were a marriage doctor what would you prescribe for your marriage in order for it to be as healthy, happy and meaningful as you would like it to be; better communication, more effective conflict resolution? More sexual intimacy? What else? Brace yourself. We're going to get intimate.

The context of our conversation was that I was getting ready to leave on a business trip for five days. It had been several days since we'd been intimate, and if we didn't make love in the next hour, it wasn't going to happen for a while. Time was short. It was decision time. Make love now, or be sex camels for the next week. Since we take sexual intimacy seriously as a way to nurture and protect our marriage we began a serious discussion. The particular situation is a significant memory because it showed both of us that we were willing to put the needs of the other ahead of our own, and that we had integrated the concept of US (our union as a couple) into our thinking about how to protect our marriage.

"Jill, I don't want to make love until it can be the way you like it, with plenty of time for conversation, taking it slow with no possibility of interruptions," I said.

I was honestly trying to love her by putting her needs ahead of my own, so her refusal was surprising.

"Jeff, you're right. Ideally I would like to wait, but I'd rather do

it now than not at all. The reality is that our schedules the next few days aren't going to cooperate with the ideal. You're going to be gone. It's now or never. **I'd rather that we both compromise in order to do something good for our marriage.** *Intimacy is important. Let's do what's good for our marriage, not just what's good for one of us."*

This sounds too good to be true, right? Well, it hasn't always been this way. We've struggled mightily in many areas of marriage including intimacy. Thankfully, we've made progress. *The key concept to which we have finally submitted after decades of marriage is this,* **the oneness of our marriage is more important than either of us as individuals.** In other words, our US is more important than our respective I's (or individual selves) (see Genesis 2:24). Very often in marriage self must die so that US can live. This is the basis for us to continually ask, *"What does our marriage need?"*

What's US?

US means the oneness of marriage, the synergistic union of two individuals and an entirely separate and superior entity compared to the two individuals that comprise the marriage.[31]

The concept of US fits nicely with the principle that the marriage is the client. When individuals step back to get perspective on the fact that together they form another entity (US), it becomes that much easier to coach the marriage. In addition to asking one another what they think, feel and want, they can also ask what the marriage needs to be healthy and happy for the duration.

In Marriage Coaching, the idea of the marriage being the client flows easily from the first question we ask couples. *"If God wants to give you a miracle for your marriage, would you be willing to receive it?"* We use this question to help to make the point that Marriage Coaching is about the marriage relationship (i.e., the US or oneness of the couple) and to activate the faith dimension to help couples to envision the kind of marriage that God wants them to have for His purposes.

Another advantage of viewing marriage as a combined entity is the quality of effort partners will make for their marriage instead of each other. We've found that couples are often more willing to try to change for their marriage than they are for their partner, especially when there are grievances, hurt or mistrust.

One of our clients, Karen, said that when she got the point about their marriage being the client that it made all the difference.

"Bill and I have been married for twenty years. We have a lot of history together. But most of it has been bad. He's admittedly been very selfish, and I've been the only one trying most of the time. I'm done. There's nothing left in my tank, but now he wants to try. He's scared that I'm acting like I don't care anymore. He's right. I don't! And until last week I'll admit that I haven't been trying. The skills you've given us are terrific, but I haven't been using them because I haven't wanted to try for him! But trying for the marriage is something entirely different. It changes everything. While I don't feel like I love Bill and I'm having a hard time respecting him, I do respect marriage and believe that it is about something bigger than him or me. And so I'm willing to try for our marriage."

Here's an analogy in case you're struggling with this idea. Consider the Office of the President of the United States. There have been some Presidents that I would be more excited to meet than others because of my views on political issues and there are some that I respect more than others. But, the fact is that if I was invited to the White House to meet a President, I would go, be polite and behave courteously out of respect for the *Office* of the President. The same is true for marriage. It is an entity that we can decide to respect by exhibiting the behavior of love, and committed effort even when we don't feel like it.[32]

Doing the right things for your marriage, even when you don't feel like it is often where restoration of pleasure begins. Persistence in loving behavior, as an act of respect for your marriage, might be the key to ignite pleasure in your relationship if you happen to be feeling stagnant or in pain. A willingness to act in faith, to do what's good for one's marriage has been a key for scores of couples we've served.

The point is that love and respect for entities beyond us can motivate us to reach deeper and try harder than compared to matters of individual interests. Consider Jesus. He didn't suffer and die for Himself, but for others; the collective "We," the *Ecclesia*, The Church which is His Bride.[33]

Math in Marriage Coaching

Since the marriage is the client, as you coach your own marriage it is important that you are mindful of the mathematical principle that what is done to one side of a math equation must be done to the other side, too. Both sides must receive equal attention, and equal treatment. With respect to the fact that in Marriage Coaching your marriage is the client this means that both partners must have equal opportunity to share their honest thoughts, feelings and desires. This requires careful self-monitoring as a couple when you are coaching your own marriage or monitoring by a Marriage Coaching Couple when coaching another marriage so that so that the ideal of "equal treatment" is a reality in the Marriage Coaching process.

For couples, it means that when you go about coaching your own marriage, you must play fair! You can't hog the spotlight by making the conversation all about you all the time! You have to make space for your partner to share, or they won't want to play. Remember how you felt in a team sport where one player hogged the ball? I don't know about you, but that made me not want to play anymore. I wanted a turn. How much more so in marriage?

Conversational Generosity

What this means practically is that as partners you need to be intentional about sharing the amount of time you take to speak and listen to each other. When we coach couples this is initially something that we facilitate very carefully, but later the couple learns to monitor on their own. As couples practice, they relax into the reality that their turn will come and that they don't have to press or compete to get the opportunity to share their thoughts, feelings and desires. This becomes self-reinforcing, meaning that it increasingly becomes something that both of you will want to do as you experience the benefit of higher quality conversations in which you feel better understood and grow closer through shared understanding.

Emotional issues are especially challenging to mediate, but the principle that the marriage is the client holds true, and the process of facilitating shared air-time to speak and listen is still effective. In fact, this is an especially important principle to practice during emotional conversations since both partners are likely to have strong feelings and/or a lot of feelings about a challenging topic. Honoring the marriage as the client means that both of you work hard not just to express yourself, but to help your partner express themselves. That might be one of the hardest things you do in Marriage Coaching conversations, especially if you disagree with their perspective, but the health of the oneness of your marriage depends on the willingness of both of you to invest tremendous energy and effort on behalf of the marriage. Remember how Karen was willing to hang in there for the marriage even if not for her husband?

Patience in the Process

The way that issues are talked about (process) is more important than the content. Remember, this is in the context of honoring your marriage as the object of your efforts. Just as you would behave with proper decorum during a visit to the office of The President of the United States, so it is imperative to engage the process of coaching your own marriage with ample patience and good-will. While we know that the content of any marriage is important, if you will honor good process you will be able to help your marriage as a helper and not just as a participant.

Patience, kindness, humility and quality listening go a long way toward building and protecting a relationship no matter the content.

Taking time to use a good process will strengthen and protect your relationship. Think about it. *If you had confidence that your spouse would receive anything that you want to share with them with patience, kindness and respect, how would that affect you?* Time after time, we see (and personally experience) pleasurable and effective sharing when partner's attitudes are patient, kind and respectful.

The quickest path through complex issues in marriage is marked by a loving attitude demonstrated in skillful asking and loving listening in our conversations.[34]

Some couples initially feel like such conversations move too slowly. They often ask, *"Are we going to get to _____ (an issue important to them)."* *"Absolutely,"* we respond. *"If it's a problem for you, then it's a problem for them (their spouse), because it's a problem for the marriage."* We quickly look to their partner to say the converse, *"And if something is problematic or painful for you, then it's a problem for me, because it's a problem for the marriage."*

Again, the marriage is the client, so issues important to both partners in the marriage are treated as equally important in the Marriage Coaching process. But even if the content is being moved through slowly, don't lose sight of the fact that you are making important progress for your marriage by the WAY you are having these discussions.

The WAY you have conversations is as important, if not more important than the content.

The Importance of Debriefings

Jill and I had just finished a difficult conversation about one of our most challenging topics; parenting. *"How would you rate the quality of our conversation?"* I asked after we were done talking. *"Like on a scale of 1-10."* I wanted to know what Jill thought about what we did well and what could be improved.

"A seven or eight, I think," she said. *"I know that parenting can be an emotional topic for us, so I think we did well with patient listening, and we took turns to completely hear each other. But I wouldn't say*

it was a ten because I shut down a little bit when you gave me a look like you were frustrated with one of my ideas. I would have liked to be able to share that without feeling like you didn't want to hear it."

"Yeah, I know," I said. *"I'm sorry, but I do think that we did pretty well overall. I appreciate you hearing me, and that you recognized that I worked hard to listen. Maybe next time I can do even better by working on my non-verbals."*

Such conversation about our conversations helps to identify what was good and what could be improved in terms of process. In the business world this is known as continuous quality improvement; the process of evaluating the way things are done that affirms that which is good, and identifies what can be improved. We use it in business to improve the bottom line of profitability, so why not do it in our relationships to improve pleasure and sustainability? Since your marriage is the client, continuous quality improvement makes sense.

Talking About Talking

Jill and I used to charge into conversations without giving much thought to the conditions around the conversation. The negative consequences of poorly planned conversations taught us to think ahead and to arrange optimum conditions for great conversations. Now, more than ever in our 29 years of dating and marriage, we practice more courtesy than ever before. And it all starts with a simple question: *"Is this a good time to talk?"*

Think about your life in the business world for a minute. Would you agree that you and your colleagues are more courteous around your conversations during the workday than at home?

I really appreciate the courtesy of being asked, *"Is this a good time to talk?"* when colleagues and clients call. Before assuming that I am available to focus on their needs they respectfully ask if I am agreeable to having a conversation. I especially like it when they introduce the conversation with parameters, *"I need five minutes to ask you a few questions,"* or, *"I estimate that we'll need 15 minutes."* It takes less than thirty seconds to understand their request and to decide if I can be my best. If not, we schedule a mutually agreeable time to have the conversation.

How many misunderstandings, arguments and hurt feelings could be avoided by practicing this simple courtesy in our homes?

Common Courtesy

In our marriage, we've noticed that the longer we live together the more liberties we're apt to take in conversations, but the result isn't good. The less time we take to consider how we are going to have a conversation the less likely we are to practice the manners that we used while dating.[35] Do you identify with this? Sometimes I try to have quick conversations without listening well to Jill because I am tired, distracted or have a low energy level. Equally, she'll admit that sometimes she tries to talk with me about complex or emotional topics before considering if the conditions are good for such a demanding conversation. Here's the point: *A few moments spent to assess if it is a good time to talk and to set the parameters for the conversation can save hours of painful disconnection.*

Jill to Jeff: *"Honey, is this a good time to talk? Or if not now, when would be? I need to talk to you about Carly (our daughter). It's probably going to take about 20 minutes because I want to tell you what I think, and I want to know how you feel. Oh, and it might be upsetting to you."*

Notice what Jill did:
1. She asked if it would be a good time to talk.
2. She estimated the amount of time it would take.
3. She alerted me to the possibility of me feeling upset.

Again, I really appreciate knowing what I'm being asked for. It puts me in a position to evaluate if I have the ability at that time to be my best because her request is clear (i.e., duration and topic). When I know specifically what Jill wants I'm better able to meet her needs, and it helps us to both honor our marriage as an entity deserving respect and a quality process.

Energy Management

Energy is an often overlooked factor in relationships. I'm not sure why this is, especially because relationships and the conversations that build them are sometimes very emotionally and mentally demanding. Elite athletes and other top performers (musicians, speakers, executives, etc.) pay careful attention to energy management and conservation. They know that they need peak levels in all domains to be their best. The same is true for relationships. Preparing to be our best for marital conversations honors the entity of our marriage as the central object of our efforts.[36]

When we talk about talking before we have conversations it puts us in a good position to take stock of our mental and emotional reserves to determine if we have enough fuel in the tank to be our best in the way we listen and respond. *Can I serve Jill well right now? Will I be able to turn off the conversation in my head and to table distractions so that I can really hear her thoughts and feelings? Am I sharp enough and emotionally rested well enough to handle the upset and to also moderate what I say?* On a very practical note, low blood sugar, dehydration and physical fatigue (lack of sleep) are all very important considerations in determining when to have a conversation.

Self-awareness about the conditions we need to have great conversations is essential. Personal comfort needs such as hunger, thirst or needing to go to the bathroom should be satisfied before we try to give our best mental, emotional and spiritual energies to those we love. Such needs are easily explained. *"I would like to grab a bit to eat and get something to drink before we begin our conversation so that I will be undistracted. You are important to me, and I really want us to be able to have a great conversation."* When Jill explains such needs to me in the context of her wanting to be her best during our conversation, I am happy to wait for her to be ready. Plus, our experience proves that a few minutes in preparation can save hours of pain and frustration!

When we coach marriages we are careful to arrive for the appointment rested, fed, and undistracted. Of course! The couple's marriage is our client! Why wouldn't we treat our own marriage with the same respect by preparing to be our best for our own marriage coaching conversations?

Jill and I often talk about the conditions we prefer in order to give our best as marriage coaches. Usually the conversation lands on the importance of reducing stress and not trying to do so much that we arrive at appointments harried and stressed. Clients deserve our best! And so does your marriage when you are trying to coach it. Time and again we see couples make quick progress toward their goals by simply reducing the stress and busyness of their lives. Fewer activities and fewer taxing and stressful activities results in more quality energy in their tanks for their marriage.

This may sound like pie in the sky to some who read this because you can't easily see where you might be able to say no to something in order to say a louder yes to your marriage. That might be one of your first goals when you begin coaching your own marriage: to make more time for your relationship. At this point let's rest on this point: When it comes to honoring your marriage as the object of your efforts in marriage coaching, *very often less is more*. (i.e., less energy drains on each of you means more for your marriage).

Consider these suggestions when you talk about talking:
When you are the one requesting a conversation:
1. Offer information about the topic(s) you want to discuss.
2. Estimate the duration, and ask for a specific amount of time.
3. Inform the person(s) if the conversation is time-sensitive (i.e., deadline).
4. Be prepared to accommodate the other person's schedule if they ask to wait.

When you are being asked for a conversation:
1. Ask yourself if you have the time and mental and emotional capacity at that time.
2. Anticipate needs that may come up during the conversation (e.g., restroom, thirst).
3. Accommodate the request right away, if possible.
4. Ask for time to reflect/pray on the topic(s), especially if potentially inflammatory.

Finally, even if we talk about talking to create ideal conditions for a great conversation we still might run into difficulty. When that happens consider taking a time-out to pray, collect your thoughts, to cool off emotionally and even to journal (See Appendix A, Time-outs for Marriage Moments). The point is to do whatever it takes to give you and your spouse (or your child, friend, etc.) the best opportunity to have a great conversation. *Remember, the quality of our relationships is directly related to the quality of our conversations.* And as your client, your marriage is worth the effort.

CHAPTER THREE
Reflection Questions:

1. What do you like about the idea of treating your marriage as your client; as the object of your efforts?

_____

_____

_____

_____

_____

2. Which tips in the second half of the chapter have potential to be helpful in your marriage?

_____

_____

_____

_____

_____

3. How balanced is the math equation in your marriage? Which side of the equation currently receives the most attention; you or your partner? What could each of you start or stop doing that would bring more balance to the equation?

_____

_____

_____

_____

_____

Essential Ingredients for a Great Marriage

A common recipe for homemade bread calls for flour, salt, sugar, water, yeast, and oil. Eliminate any of these items, and the mixture isn't bread. Every ingredient is necessary. None can be forgotten. Bread isn't bread unless all the components are present, mixed together in the right combination, and baked for a specific amount of time.

The same is true for a great marriage. Several key ingredients are required to build and sustain a great marriage relationship that is full of hope, joy and purpose. *The essential ingredients to develop and sustain a great marriage are* **heart, hope and skills.**

To successfully coach your own marriage it is essential to use effective skills and to do helpful exercises with a heart of love and to hope in faith for more and better in your relationship. Both heart and hope are gifts of God through an authentic relationship with Jesus, so two-thirds of what you need comes from Him, not other people, including your spouse.

Once these are established, skills will help you to steward relationship healing and strengthening opportunities because skills and exercises are the channels through which your love and hope are given to your partner, and through which your partner can express their hopeful love to you.

The Essential Ingredients

Our *Heart* is the well-spring of our deepest desires, and the source of compassion, forgiveness and grace. The heart we need in order to develop and sustain a godly marriage is the heart of Jesus, which is compassionate, selfless, patient, self-controlled, and so much more.

The Bible describes Jesus as a man who came not to be served but to serve, "*For even the Son of Man did not come to be served, but to serve, and to give his life as a ransom for many."* (Mark 10:45), who put the needs of others ahead of his own, *"Do nothing out of selfish ambition or vain conceit. Rather, in humility value others above yourselves, not looking to your own interests but each of you to the interests of the others,"* (Philippians 2:3, 4), and who was able to maintain emotional control when mistreated by others, *"When they hurled their insults at him, he did not retaliate; when he suffered, he made no threats. Instead, he entrusted himself to him who judges justly."* (I Peter 2:23).

The heart we need to build and sustain abundant marriage is not something we can establish in ourselves. Rather, it is imparted to us by God through relationship with Jesus, cultivated and sustained through intimate familiarity with His life and His heart; His thoughts, feelings and desires. Think about it. How would it be for your husband/wife to be married to a person who embodies the heart of Jesus? To what degree are you like Him?

It is an ongoing process to become Christ-like, but we don't have to wait until a certain degree of His likeness is formed in us to love our spouses the way He loves. We can grow in every conversation. For example, the heart of Jesus can be touched by a listener through prayer before and during conversations: *Lord, please help me to hear with your ears, see with your eyes and feel with your heart. I want to be like you as I listen. In Jesus' name. Amen.*

Hope has a spiritual basis too. While failures and pain can threaten to extinguish it, it only takes a shred of hope to try in relationships, again and again. *"Now faith is confidence in what we hope for and assurance about what we do not see"* (Hebrews 11:1). Hope is future oriented. It is about something that it not yet a reality. When a couple envisions what can be and what they would like to be the future reality of their marriage, they are demonstrating faith according to this definition. Look at it again, *"Now faith is confidence in what we hope for..."* Couples sometimes express faith in words like this, *We have confidence that this process is going to work for us. We have faith in what you are teaching us. We've done other hard things in life, so we think we can do this too.*

Skills provide effective ways to hold other's hearts when they dare to share their honest thoughts, feelings and desires. Skills provide specific ways for partners to express themselves and to clearly hear each other. Skills are often used in exercises that have a beginning and ending point for the expression of thoughts, feelings and desires.

We haven't seen a couple fail to accomplish their goals when they persevere in their relationship with the powerful combination of these three ingredients. However, the absence of even one of these can mean the difference between success and failure of couples to develop and sustain an abundantly hopeful, pleasurable and purposeful marriage.

When Ingredients are Missing

One: heart without hope is short-lived goodwill.
Either one partner, or both, has a teachable and humble heart, but lack hope in God or each other. So much water is under the bridge of their relationship that they can't imagine it ever being different in the future.

Ann discovered that Andy had two affairs for a total duration of six years. She had little hope that he would change. During initial Marriage Coaching sessions she stated her willingness to accept her part of the relationship problems, but was lacking hope that her efforts would make a difference. She'd hoped before and gotten burned. It appeared to us that Andy was trying, but simply couldn't live down years of deception in a matter of weeks, and he wasn't very skillful in his ability to listen to and hear his wife, or to express his own thoughts and feelings. This was a critical point in the process. It could have gone either way. The combination of Andy's past behavior and his lack of skillful listening could have meant the end of their marriage. Sadly, in some marriages that is exactly what we've seen. But this marriage was about to take a miraculous turn for the better.

Ann asked us to hope with her for her marriage. In faith we believed and prayed with her for a change in Andy's heart and that he would learn skills to help them to communicate better. We demonstrated faith to Andy by supporting and encouraging him as he tried to use new skills to hear Ann and to express himself. As he listened more effectively he became sincerely remorseful and asked for forgiveness. Ann experienced him as sincere.

Ultimately, good skills made it possible for Andy to hear Ann's broken heart and to express his remorseful heart. She needed him to see and hear how she'd been affected by his infidelity before she would allow her heart to hope for complete reconciliation. Hope for the marriage grew and was sustained through repeated use of good skills with heart.

Two: heart without skills is humble ignorance.

A good analogy is an athlete who has a strong, competitive heart, and willingness to learn, but loses in competition because their raw talent and desire hasn't been shaped for expression through sport-specific skills.

Susanna and Tim wanted to communicate more effectively about step-parenting issues. Time and again they'd tried in ways they knew, but continued to break down in their talks before reaching agreements. The parents were at odds and the kids were confused. They were willing to try to make things different but they needed effective ways to express their thoughts, feelings and desires to each other and to set and pursue goals.

They did try differently after learning to use the basic skills of the coaching process. First they worked through the emotional hurt that both of them had experienced from each other by taking turns speaking and listening and then forgiving each other. Then they worked through a coaching funnel process to identify a shared goal for their parenting. Finally, they successfully worked as a team to brainstorm action-steps to accomplish their goal. All throughout the process they continued with good heart and hope. Their efforts were successful in making changes in their parenting this time because they had the skills to honor the desires of their hearts to do differently in their partnership as parents. They'd always been humble enough to see the need to parent as a team in a different way, but now they were no longer ignorant about how to effectively communicate to set and attain a shared goal.

Three: hope without heart or skills is an unachievable dream.

This combination is comparable to fantasy. This type of couple has abundant hope but lack heart to persist in learning. The result is that they miss out on an opportunity to learn to use skills to make their dreams for their relationship a reality. Couples in this category call to schedule a complimentary consultation, but then proceed to tell us how our approach won't work (before they try). After listening to our description of the process and impressive outcome data (an 89% stay-together rate)[37] some confide honestly that while the approach sounds good, that their heart isn't into the investment of time, money and energy required for a possible positive outcome. This is one of the saddest situations we see; couples in pain, hopeless, and sometimes lacking in the humility necessary to try to learn something new and to do things in a different way.

Four: skill without heart is manipulation.

This is the proverbial resounding gong or clanging cymbal of 1 Corinthians 13. All the knowledge in the world is useless unless applied with love. Our partners know when our heart is behind the use of a skill such as active listening, and when we are just doing the skill without sincerity and humility.

George really showed himself in our coaching sessions by actively listening with a sarcastic tone of voice, then protesting that he'd done as well as he could. Thelma pointed out his lack of good-hearted effort. He eventually admitted that he'd not made his best effort in coaching appointments or at home between coaching sessions. Eventually he admitted that he had participated in the sessions with an agenda to feign effort so that he could save face with friends and family members by telling them that he'd tried his best. The story could have ended there. Sometimes it does. But George eventually called to report that our confrontation in their final session about the absence of his heart eventually convicted him. At that point he began to engage the process of healing his marriage with heart, and they were still together![38]

Five: skill without hope is useless knowledge.

Sam and Diane wanted to learn skills but refused to allow for a miracle from God. They admitted that they felt hopeless, and that they didn't want to ask God for a miracle. They were done! But, they felt obligated to save face with their pastor by agreeing to see us to learn how to communicate and approach conflict differently. Still, they weren't willing to confess their shortcomings and hopelessness. Sadly, they wouldn't even try skills in our presence. This was unfortunate because they might have had a pleasurable experience of being heard and understood. They were bright people who had the ability to learn essential concepts and skills very quickly, but had no hope or heart for change. They came only once and gave an unfair report to their pastor that that coaching couple didn't know how to help us. To the contrary! They didn't try!

Putting it all Together

Any couple with hope for more and better in their marriage can benefit from a coaching approach to growth or healing as part of their recipe for a healthier, more whole, and more pleasurable and purposeful marriage. The most successful process we have witnessed began in God-affected hearts that were humble to learn and grow by doing whatever it took to make their marriage what God wanted it to be.

During the journey of being coached, or coaching one's own marriage we find that once hope and heart are in place, skills facilitate the growth and change that God initiated. If you think that you or your partner are missing one or more essential ingredients take heart! All is not lost! Heart can be cultivated, hope can be ignited, and skills can be learned and mastered.

If heart is absent our recommendation is to cultivate a relationship with Jesus Christ as your Savior and Lord. Consider His heart toward those He influenced and ministered to in the Bible, and ask Him to cultivate His heart within you.

When hope is missing we encourage you to pray for faith to envision what can be and what God wants to be in your marriage. This isn't what you can imagine based on what has taken place before, but fresh and unreasonable vision that is in the realm of dreams. What would be mind-boggling to you, your spouse, family and friends if it was the reality of your marriage? What would your marriage be like if it was a relationship to die for? Remember, God can do immeasurably more than we can ask or imagine (See Ephesians 3:20).

Deficits in skills are the easiest ingredient to remedy. All that is required is simple learning and practice to the point that your use of them becomes second nature. Until that point, rely on rules and procedures for the use of skills in exercises with specific guidelines for their use.

A Journey of Healing

Look for the ways that the following scenario was completely transformed from hopelessness to hope, pain to pleasure, and aimlessness to purpose. Note how the essential ingredients of heart, hope and skills were cultivated and combined for a successful outcome, and then prayerfully imagine how these same ingredients might combine for a similar outcome in your relationship!

Ted and Cindy came for Marriage Coaching as a final effort to avoid a painful future for themselves and their children. They were separated and she and her attorney were poised to execute a divorce. Nate's gambling and repeated lies had eroded trust and squandered family assets. They agreed about their chances of survival; minus 20 on a scale of 0 to 100.

They came initially only to honor the request of a friend they trusted. Their response to their friend's request was, *"What harm can it do when we both think the marriage is already dead?"* Cindy admitted that her heart was hard. Ted was broken and remorseful. *"You don't know what you've got until it's gone,"* he said. Their physical separation foreshadowed the kind of pain they believed they would experience in the future. Ted's comment was that, *"The time I've been away from my kids, and the nights on my friend's couch have been the most miserable days of my life."*

This broken and desperate couple didn't have any skills to dialogue about pain, anger, sadness and fear. They had tried an approach with a counselor that wasn't helping because it didn't help them to deal with their emotions in a constructive way. They didn't know how to talk about the language of the heart (emotions), and the tools the counselor put in their hands served more as weapons than aids to build bridges. *"In that approach all we did was cut each other up by venting our mutually angry and resentful feelings."*

When you're sliding down the face of an icy mountain toward oblivion like Ted and Cindy, it is imperative to get a grip on anything that might slow or arrest your slide. An instinct for survival is all it takes to motivate you to grab for anything that might save your marriage. Your effort might be fueled by a dim ray of hope to survive, or a compassionate heart for others involved in the situation (e.g., children, parents, or friends) that would be affected by the death of your relationship. But the important thing is to try to get a grip to stop your slide into the abyss.

Often, in our experience, it is a skill or exercise that gives a couple something to hold on to, so the lifeline we offered to Ted and Cindy was a skillfully facilitated conversation about feelings in which they each had opportunity to speak and be heard. We prompted them to actively listen to each other about their honest thoughts and feelings in a sequence that began with anger and moved through sadness and fear. By the end of the conversation they surprised themselves by expressing some pleasurable feelings, including things about which they were hopeful. It was amazing and moving to watch.

Note that Ted and Cindy's slide off the cliff was interrupted at first by a skill. Simple effective listening with heart and skill provided a foothold from which they could recover their marriage. The very first time they used this skill they began learning to coach their own marriage. This is supported by the fact that they chose to use the skill at home during conversations when we weren't present.

Near the end of this first session Cindy said, *"That conversation went better than it ever has before. It gives me a ray of hope for us."* Cindy's hope gave Ted hope. Soon they both began to imagine what else they might be able to talk about in a more productive way. Then they made a rank-ordered list of issues. This was fine with us, of course, because in coaching, the client sets the agenda. As hope grew through more conversations that went well, humble hearts began to emerge. Both partners began to confess attitudes and behaviors that they knew had bothered the other. That led to the appearance of repentant hearts in which they specifically confessed things they knew had hurt each other and then asked forgiveness. On and on it went, in an *upward* spiral!

While it is indisputable that Ted and Cindy's marriage was on life support when they first came to us, they at least had a faint heartbeat of hope. This was evident in their humility to try new ways of communicating. It was especially easy to convince them to try something different because the way they were trying before was only adding to the pain.

Activities to Develop Heart, Hope and Skills

We've found that the single most powerful demonstration in Marriage Coaching training is selfless listening to one another about ways that we have offended or hurt each other. Audiences get deathly quiet when we do this. Sometimes they seem to literally hold their breath. Why? Because they expect the partner who is being confronted to break ranks with the process to selfishly defend, rationalize or to make a counter-accusation. That's the common way that such conversations happen behind closed doors, right?

Think about original sin. God confronts Adam about eating from the tree of knowledge of good and evil. What does Adam do? He blames the woman. He didn't humbly say, *"You're right. I'm sorry. Will you forgive me?"* No. Such humility in the face of confrontation isn't natural. Thus, when we model unnatural humility and selflessness for our trainees we're actually modeling godly love. *That, in a nutshell is the power of the Christian Coaching approach to marriage; it models Christ-like love.* **The skills simply give us the opportunity to model His love.** Here are some ways that you might put yourselves in a position to grow your heart, hope and skills.

Heart

Here is what we say to couples in Level III Marriage Coaching training classes (these couples are hand selected for their character and abilities to train other couples in Marriage Coaching):

> *"Anyone can teach skills, but only those of us that are being continually transformed by the selfless love of Christ can authentically convey a genuine selfless posture of our heart in relationship to our spouse. Whether we do this in person with a single couple, by phone or in a live seminar for scores of couples, each time we lay ourselves aside to hear our spouse's honest thoughts, feelings and desires, we effectively show Jesus' love to the world. Habitual selflessness is a posture of the heart that makes skills effective. Thus, it is such selflessness, humble and authentic willingness to hold our partner's heart, rather than attempting to assert for ourselves, that is the most powerful concept to teach through lecture and modeling for others."*

And so, such selflessness empowered by godly love (the I Corinthians 13 kind of love) is an imperative ingredient in your pursuit of an abundantly hopeful, pleasurable and purposeful marriage.

Here's a powerful exercise to measure the depth and quality of your heart. Perhaps you've done it before. Grab a Bible to read I Corinthians 13. Focus specifically on verses 4-7. Now take a moment to reflect on the kind of love that is described. Make notes on your observations in this passage. Second, pray for insight about application of this to you. Ask God where He would have you grow in this type of love. Write down what comes to mind.

Now, for a third and final step: Re-read the passage, but this time, insert your name in place of the word love. For example:

"Jeff is patient, Jeff is kind. Jeff does not envy, Jeff does not boast, Jeff is not proud. Jeff does not dishonor others, Jeff is not self-seeking, Jeff is not easily angered, and Jeff keeps no record of wrongs. Jeff

does not delight in evil but rejoices with the truth. Jeff always protects, always trusts, always hopes, and always perseveres."

Now, ask yourself, Am I? Do I? To what extent is this true of me? Your answers provide you with ideas for how to coach yourself in the development of a Christ-like heart.

Hope

Absence of hope is a painful experience. Tragically, it is one of the last emotional experiences for persons who die by suicide. It is very sad that for them the future seems devoid of any possibility for things to be different. This is also what many couples in pain experience. They describe hopelessness when offered an opportunity to heal their marriage, "We can't imagine things ever being different."

In the natural, the best predictor of the future is the past. What people have done is what they will continue to do, unless something changes, or someone intervenes. This is exactly why one of our favorite questions for couples in pain is the miracle question, *"If God wants to give you a miracle for your marriage, would you be willing to receive it?"* This question is effective because it jolts couples into the realm of faith which is described as hope for that which is not yet seen or experienced (Hebrews 11:1).[39]

Remember, hope in faith is one of the three essential ingredients to attain and sustain an abundantly pleasurable and purposeful marriage. But again, hope is something that no person can impart to you. Rather, God who gives the gift of faith is the giver of this essential perspective about what He wants to be for your marriage.

So, here's the exercise. It's simple yet incredibly potent.

Ask God to give you a vision for what your marriage can be. Pray, *"God, please show me/us what you want for our marriage."* Then watch and listen for pictures, ideas and words or phrases that the Lord brings to your awareness. In addition, give liberty to your imagination to think about your best dreams for your marriage. What do you see yourselves doing together, and how do you feel in those experiences?

What do you hear from your spouse and see him/her doing in your best dreams?

Your reaction might be, *That will never happen.* Now ask who would want you to believe that thought. It isn't God. Such beliefs are faith killers. By definition, faith is being sure of what you hope for and certain of that which you don't yet see. This might be the single-most challenging and difficult ingredient of Marriage Coaching, and the most important; a willingness to hope for that which you don't currently see or experience (faith). Now, understand that once you are willing to take the unreasonable step of hoping in faith, that God sees your step and that He will honor it by giving you the courage to keep walking toward the vision He has given you.

Skills

Finally, the recipe of essential ingredients calls for skills. These provide a channel for your heart to be experienced by your partner, and they are the tools that God can use to build the dream that He has for your marriage.

Skills are state of the art tools that are necessary to create relationship masterpieces. Compare Michelangelo's use of paint brushes to tools and skills such as effective listening, asking and goal-setting. When such tools are wielded by loving, compassionate and unselfish partners in faith then the product of their efforts will be a wonder of beauty like the ceiling of the Sistine Chapel.

Let's get practical about tools and skills. *If you and your spouse could custom-design a tool to accomplish something essential for your marriage, what would it do?* Take a moment to give your mind an opportunity for a creative response. After you have an answer or two, or if you are stuck, take a look at some of the responses we've heard.

"It would be like a stethoscope that I could put on my wife's heart that would tell me exactly how she is feeling so that I don't misunderstand when she explains it to me.

It would be some kind of shaker that we would both put our desires into. Shake it up and out comes that perfect solution to the dilemma of both of us getting our needs met.

It would be something that would help us to de-escalate emotional conversations so that we can have a rational discussion and then negotiate a compromise."

Sometimes you will be able to reach into your existing toolbox to pull out a very specifically crafted tool that will do exactly what your marriage needs. And sometimes you will get creative. The point is to persevere in the process of expressing your heart with skill in hopes that the vision will become reality day by day.

Summary

Look back to the beginning of I Corinthians 13. Without love we are resounding gongs and clanging cymbals; a lot of noise and ruckus without much focused product. But with love, we are powerful and potent to the lives we touch. Thus, this in-depth focus on the essential foundation of ingredients was necessary. You have to have a deep and adequate foundation of Christ's heart, faith and effective tools and skills to cooperate with the Master Builder in the process of making your marriage what He wants it to be. Please remember and return to these ingredients as you download details on the skills and processes that come next. We will continue to emphasize specific aspects of heart as we go, but mostly you will be learning (or perhaps re-learning) specific skills in the next few chapters.

CHAPTER FOUR
Reflection Questions:

1. Evaluate yourself on each of the three essential ingredients. How much heart, hope and skill do you have for your marriage? Rate each on a scale (1-10) and then support your answer. For instance, if you answer five for hope, say what is present that makes it a five and then talk about what isn't present yet since it isn't a 10.

_____

_____

_____

_____

_____

2. Which of the five descriptions of a missing ingredient best describes your marriage in the past or presently? Brainstorm five things you could do build all three ingredients into your relationship.

_____

_____

_____

_____

_____

3. Name one part of Ted and Cindy's story that stands out to you. Why? How did their story impact you?

_____

_____

_____

_____

_____

CHAPTER FIVE

How to Coach Your Marriage?

The rest of the book will teach you to coach your own marriage. You can begin while you read this chapter by following the recommended steps. But first, let's listen in on a couple as they coach their marriage to give you an idea of what this might sound like in your marriage.

"Honey, what do you think our marriage needs?" Jack asked Marilyn.

"Fun," she said. *"Definitely more fun; like we used to enjoy just relaxing and laughing together, but there hardly seems to be time for that now, with the kid's schedules and all."*

Jack realized that this would be a good time to try to listen effectively. *"Honey, I think I hear you saying that you would like us to make time to enjoy each other like we used to; that you really miss that,"* he offered tentatively.

"Exactly," she said enthusiastically. *"But you know what else I think,"* Marilyn continued. *"I think our marriage needs time that is protected from anything or anyone else. We're blessed with a great life and great friends, but we're so spontaneous about accepting offers to do things with people that some weeks we don't end up with much time together, and I miss that. Our opportunities for intimacy sometimes evaporate when one of us says yes to a friend's invitations to do good things and fun things like the barbecue the Smith's planned at the last minute Saturday. That was great, but I thought we were going to have the evening to ourselves. I think our marriage needs more time alone."*

Jack summarized in his own words again, *"I think that you are saying that you felt disappointed that I accepted Bob's invitation to the barbecue before checking with you because you had different hopes for the evening; that it had been awhile since we'd had time alone at home without the kids, and you were looking forward to it just being us?"*

"Yes, that's the gist of it Jack. Thank you. What do you think? Do you want more time for us too? Or is it just me?" Marilyn asked.

"I agree," Jack said. *"I'm sorry that I accepted that invitation before checking with you. Maybe our marriage needs the rule that we check with each other about invitations that involve both of us or that would have an impact on each other."*

Marilyn looked happy. *"Yes, that sounds good."*

How realistic is it for your marriage to have a conversation like this? Some who read this will see immediate potential for problems because when you make requests for change to your partner, it is taken as criticism. That's where the ingredients of heart and hope come in. Our suggestion is to pray for loving patience to do the process with good-will and hope in faith that such conversations can go differently for you. The experience of a multitude of couples is that the more they practice the process, the more they trust it and the less likely they are to short-circuit it with defensiveness.

If you have difficulty imagining such a conversation in your marriage, take heart! We have seen rapid growth for couples who want to grow and change, who give God room to do miracles, and who are willing to take one step at a time, in faith, that more and better is possible!

Steps to Coach Your Marriage

If you're ready, get started coaching your own marriage right now! As you work through the following steps, take notes on new insights and decisions you make to improve your relationship. We recommend that you return to these steps frequently to re-assess what your marriage needs and what you can do to strengthen it.

1. **Agree to try to self-coach your marriage.**

   First, agree that you will try to coach your marriage. *Note: For a coaching approach to work you both need to be motivated to grow and change, and willing to be responsible to do the work necessary to improve your relationship.* This has to be a voluntary decision to partner together for the sake of your marriage.[40] Regardless of past efforts to heal, strengthen and protect your marriage, are you willing to try again? Are you willing to hope in faith for something better, more fulfilling, pleasurable and purposeful? If so, then coaching your own marriage might work for you.

   ### The importance of unity

   Unity is symbolized in some wedding ceremonies by the simultaneous lighting of a single candle by the bride and the groom. This represents two individuals becoming one. It is this oneness that you are working to heal, strengthen and protect.

   "That is why a man leaves his father and mother and is united to his wife, and they become one flesh." (Genesis 2:24)

   Coaching your marriage is different than two individuals having a conversation. It is a decision to respect the reality that there is a third entity that is above and beyond the individual participants. We mentioned this as the concept of your marriage being the client in chapter three. Another way to think about this is the idea of a team vs. an individual in team sports. Whereas a team player prioritizes team goals over personal goals and desires, the individualist sacrifices team for self. Ideally, in team sports there is no I or self. Thus, the best scenario for marriage is a couple that prioritizes the good of the marriage above individual interests and desires, *although these are included in the process of understanding what your marriage needs.*[41]

2.   **Ask what your marriage needs.**

Begin by each of you asking this question of yourself before comparing your answers. Steps b and c will help you to develop your answer. We suggest allowing at least 10-15 minutes for each question. It is ideal to pray, reflect and journal or take notes of your answers.

First, take a step back to look at your marriage objectively to get perspective on what it needs. Ask yourself, *"What does our marriage need?"*

Pray. Ask God, *"What would you like for our marriage?"*

Ask, *"If our marriage could speak what would it ask for?"*

Finally, ask, *"What would I like more of or less of and what would I like to start/stop happening in our marriage?"*

Asking the question of what your marriage needs is similar to taking a step back from your young children and asking what they need (more sleep, discipline, attention, etc.). Once you determine what they need you brainstorm action-steps you could do to meet their need. If you don't have children, think about your house. *"What does our house need?"*

Obviously, it is possible to ask your partner these same questions. The reason we urge you to ask yourself first is to strengthen your ability to discern for yourself, and to increase your ability to hear God as you privately pray and reflect on the needs of your marriage.

The point of this exercise is to develop the habit of looking at your marriage as something apart from yourself that has a life of its own that needs to be cared for.[42]

3. **Ask your partner what they want in your marriage and for your marriage.**

   The following questions will help you to access your partner's heart for your marriage.

   Focus on desires. *"What do you want more of and less of in our marriage? What do you want to start happening and/ or to stop happening?"*

   Focus on feelings. Ask, *"How do you feel in our marriage?"* and *"How would you like to feel in our marriage?"* Ask what they think they could do more or less or start or stop doing that would improve their feelings and yours in your marriage. Now, think about something you would like to ask for from your partner. If they ask you, what would you request from them to start/stop or to do more or less that would be helpful to your marriage?

4. **Compare your answers.**

   Look for similarities and points of agreement. The places you agree are a good place to start the process of setting a shared goal. Again, the assumption in Marriage Coaching is that you are both motivated to grow and change, and willing to take responsibility to accomplish it.

   At the very least, look for things your spouse identified that you are willing to take responsibility to work on for the sake of the marriage. Shared goals don't have to be about things you both want. They can be things that one of you wants and the other is agreeable to work on with you. And remember, the more you come to the marriage with the servant attitude of Jesus to selflessly serve others, the more you will receive back. In other words, you will reap what you sow. *When you go to give, your partner is more likely to WANT to give back to you than if you go to get.*

A note about goals: Some couples prefer to work on one goal at a time while others like to work on several goals at a time. Decide together how many goals to work on. Secondly, some couples have found that working on a fairly easy goal at first builds confidence in their ability to use the goal-setting process effectively. This is like learning the technique of lifting weights; you learn the technique with lighter weights before adding more weight.

5. **Imagine what your marriage will look like and feel like in the future.**

    This is the time-tested principle of beginning with the end in mind.[43] Ask, *"When we have accomplished the growth and change we want and that we think our marriage needs, what will that be like? What will it look like and feel like and how will that be different than what is happening now?"* Your answers to these questions are the beginning of a specific and measurable goal.

6. **Brainstorm ways you can give your marriage what it wants and what it needs.**

    Once you have some ideas about what your marriage wants and needs you can take the next step to make a plan to fulfill your desires. Ask yourselves, *"What are some possible ways we can accomplish what we want?"* This is the step of generating potential action steps to make your desires a reality. The number and quality of ideas you come up with will probably reflect the depth and breadth of your resources to work on your marriage (i.e., skills, exercises and marriage-specific information). If you come up short, don't fret. Simply continue to build your library through reading, seminars and possibly receiving Marriage Coaching from a trained couple. Know that there are a multitude of couples who have gained a lot of experience and information through their own marriage strengthening process and by helping other couples.[44]

A. Once you have your list (try to come up with at least five potential action-steps), evaluate them. Which ones do you like the most? Which ones do you think will work best? Then rank-order them according to the ones that you are most interested in doing. This process reflects the coaching principle that we are more apt to do the things we want to do than what others tell us we should do. This is your opportunity to choose action-steps that you think will work and that you are motivated to do!

B. Finally, count the cost. How long will it take to do the action-steps that you want to do? Do you want to commit to do these? If you do, then we suggest you write them on your calendar for the specific time and date(s) that you will do them.[45] In coaching we say that an action-step isn't a legitimate action-step until you have committed to a specific time and date to do it.

7. **Make time to take action.**
   Once you have some ideas in mind about things you can do to reach the goals you have set for your marriage, start doing some of them. Decide when and how long you are going to do specific action-steps. For instance, you may agree that it would be good for your marriage to share things that will build closeness and prevent misunderstandings before the workday begins. You might also agree that taking walks together is a helpful and healthy activity for your marriage because walking together provides undistracted time for your relationship and it also supports a shared goal to invest in your health through exercise. Then you might brainstorm a specific action-step. You might agree to walk together before 7:30 a.m. on weekdays

for at least 30 minutes, three times a week, and to share what you appreciate about each other and any new information while you walk. Do you see how that is a specific, measurable step that will help the overall goal to become reality?

8. **Make the process of coaching your marriage a habit.**
   Life is ever-changing. Our needs and desires are subject to change as our life circumstances change. As you develop the habit of proactively coaching your marriage (continually asking what it needs and what you want), you will constantly be strengthening and protecting your relationship by keeping pace with the ebb and flow of changes and seasons of life.

Is this step-wise process clean and easy? Or do you see challenges and pitfalls? What isn't mentioned in these eight steps is the importance of good asking and listening. Go back to the Marriage Coaching conversation of Jack and Marilyn at the beginning of this chapter. Notice how Jack carefully reflected what he heard Marilyn saying. By doing that, he ensured that he heard what she wanted him to hear, and demonstrated to her that he understood. If the conversation was more complex, there probably would have been some questions back and forth about each other's thoughts and feelings behind the requests. (We'll get to the technique of asking effective questions in chapter 7). Our point is that this conversational goal-setting process is about more than coming up with ideas to strengthen marriage; it's also about deep listening and understanding about what is in each other's hearts. Such understanding is possible as you use good skills with heart.

You now have the basic process needed to coach your own marriage. The remainder of the book will help you to further develop the necessary attitudes, skills and perspective to become excellent coaches of your own marriage.

*See Appendix B for a detailed description of the typical progression of a Marriage Coaching relationship.

CHAPTER FIVE
Reflection Questions:

1. What excites you about the potential of coaching your marriage? What scares you?

_____

_____

_____

_____

_____

2. How badly do you want to learn to coach your own marriage? Why? What is motivating you to gain this set of skills? What do you hope it can do for you that other approaches haven't?

_____

_____

_____

_____

_____

3. Which of the eight steps seems easiest? Which ones are the most challenging? What will it take for you to integrate this process into your relationship?

_____

_____

_____

_____

_____

PART II

Essential Skills to Make
Your Marriage Great!

The Heart & Skill of Effective Listening

What makes effective listening so hard? By itself, the skill is simple to teach, and simple to do. *Simply tell your partner in your own words what you heard them say after they share three-five sentences.* At the lowest level, it is repeating (parroting) what you heard your spouse say. But, just doing the skill doesn't cut it. Your partner can tell when you are merely going through the motions, utilizing the skills although you don't really seem to care.

Effective listening that is loving, selfless and respectful is as much a posture of the heart as it is a specific skill. And, heart empowered listening is potent because it invites and enables our partner to share honest thoughts, feelings and desires without fear of judgment, rejection, or ridicule.

To genuinely hear what your partner is saying requires a posture of the heart that is willing to wholly surrender and set itself aside for a period of time in order to prioritize the desires and perceptions of the other person. The bad news is that when this heart posture is absent to any degree, your marriage relationship is unlikely to be as pleasurable and purposeful as it could be. The good news is that any couple (or individual in situations where your partner isn't motivated) can grow their heart and improve their skill!

The primary reason it's hard to listen effectively is because our heart has to be involved, totally committed at a deep level of selflessness. That is the ongoing work of God in our life, to mature us into people who sacrifice our lives for the best of others. Jill and I struggle with this from time to time, but we're always able to determine the reason for our difficulties: *selfishness and pride.*

Here are common ways these culprits have shown up in our relationship:

1. We each wanted circumstances to go our way.
2. We each thought our perspective was the correct perspective.
3. The way we wanted things to happen was the way that we think things should have happened.

The primary way we kick these unwanted visitors out of our home is by both of us submitting to an authority greater than ourselves. This is where the heart work of effective listening comes in.

The basic components of listening can be spelled out in the following equation:

Prayer + Heart + Skill = Effective Listening

The Importance of Prayer

When we have attempted to effectively listen in our own marriage, we place no hope or trust in ourselves to listen from the heart even though we have been trained well and have a lot of experience. Therefore, we plead with God in prayer to go before us, to guide us, and to do fully and completely what only He can do in each of our hearts, minds and wills. As we talk and listen, we continue in prayer as we share with each other, quietly asking the Lord throughout the conversation to keep our hearts soft, selfless and attentive.

Jill and I have learned that it is time well spent to pray before we try to hear each other. Otherwise, we're apt to attempt to accomplish a pre-set agenda or to prematurely develop conclusions about the outcome. Praying to have a surrendered spirit throughout our conversations helps us to be other focused rather than self-focused. This helps us to see, hear and feel with the tenderness and selflessness of Christ.

Below is the type of prayer we say before and during conversations.

> *Lord, please help us to hear what you would have us hear. Help us to listen with your ears, feel with your heart, and see with your eyes. Please help us to enter this time of sharing with an open and hopeful heart and the realization that you are with us in this, and want us to be free to be open and honest with our thoughts, feelings and desires. You are the unseen moderator and facilitator of our communication, and we trust you to keep our minds open, and our hearts hopeful and compassionate. In Jesus' name—Amen!*

We encourage you to compose one of your own or to use this one if it works for you.

Holding Your Partner's Heart

Consider how a heart surgeon holds their patient's heart. They cradle it gently in their hands with caring skill. They are careful to not bruise, drop or otherwise damage this vital organ because the very life of their patient depends on how they handle it. Similarly, the quality of life in your marriage depends on how you hold each other's hearts.

Holding Hearts has been a remarkably compelling image for quite a few couples. We know of one couple who purchased a ceramic heart that they pass back and forth to remind them to take turns listening to each other's deepest longings, intimate thoughts, and honest feelings. This couple also says that the fact the heart is ceramic, and would shatter into a thousand pieces if dropped, reminds them to be careful and gentle in their conversation!

Holding Hearts has a double-meaning: *It is both a way of being and a set of skills.*

First, a *Holding Heart* is a specific type of person. A Holding Heart is the type of person whose inner qualities of character can be seen consistently through their compassionate and selfless attitudes and actions. Since our heart is the well-spring of our deepest desires, and the fountain of compassion, forgiveness and grace it is constantly growing and being nurtured and shaped by our spiritual beliefs, values and relationship with God.

Philippians 2:3, 4 describes the essential selflessness necessary to be a good listener. Paul urges Christ-followers to emulate the selflessness of Jesus when he says, *"Do nothing out of selfish ambition or vain conceit. Rather, in humility value others above yourselves, not looking to your own interests but each of you to the interests of the others."*

Have you ever thought that you need supernatural help to get along with your spouse? Do you ever think that you need to be like God to get along and understand? Well, here's your chance. Die to your own desires. Emulate Jesus who did not come to be served but to serve.[46] Look fully to your partner's needs. Hear them completely without considering yourself. Turn off your SELF for a few minutes and see what that does to help your relationship.

Second, ***Holding Hearts*** is what we do when we employ a specific set of skills to elicit and hold the deepest thoughts, feelings and desires of our spouse. This is the essence of intimacy; the ability and willingness to know another, and to make our true selves known in an environment of safety, appreciation and acceptance. In fact, these are the prerequisite conditions for most of us to be willing to share our hearts.

Thus, Holding Hearts refers both to a group of people that are compassionate as a function of their loving and selfless character qualities, and it is a set of skills that they employ to hear, hold and understand the innermost honest thoughts, feelings and desires of others. Simply said, Holding Hearts are a type of people that use specific skills to communicate love. The character of those that hold others hearts is recognized by humility, compassion and self-sacrifice; in a word, love.[47] Skills simply allow us to effectively express what is in our hearts.[48]

To Men:

If I was sitting with you in a Marriage Coaching session I would encourage you to listen like Jesus: *"Have you ever wondered how you could do what Paul said, to love your wife as Christ loved the Church and gave himself up for her? Well, here's your chance. Die to yourself. Hear what she has to say without interjecting what you are thinking or feeling."*

This is an incredibly important point, so I'll say it again. *Hear what she says without interjecting what you think about or how you feel about what she said.* To do this requires the discipline of turning off the conversation in your head. The evidence that we all have numerous conversations going on in our minds at any one time is found in the reality that we often lose track of conversations or forget what we've been told. This is no small problem! The human tendency to go down bunny trails in our minds significantly interferes in relationships. While others are opening their hearts to us, we're chasing a stray thought down a path that the speaker isn't going. When they notice that we aren't with them in the conversation, they become annoyed, and reasonably so! We're listening to ourselves, not them!

You can learn to shut off the conversation in your head through practice. Every conversation you have, with your spouse or another individual is an opportunity to grow as a listener. First, condition your heart to be selfless. Several strategies work for me, and you can probably think of some for yourself. I recite a few of the verses from I Corinthians 13 to remind me that I am loving, and how to love in action (i.e., patient, kind, selfless, etc.), then I relax in the conversation to hear instead of to be heard. One verse I meditate on frequently helps me to adopt Jesus' posture in relationships, "...the Son of Man did not come to be served, but to serve..." (Mark 10:45).

My paraphrase of that passage in the context of a listening opportunity goes like this, "I'm arriving in this conversation to give, not to get; to listen, not to be heard."

Some self-talk can help at this point; *this is about them, and I can love them by listening from my heart with good skill.* Another helpful reminder is that God is my Father who knows my heart and cares about my needs. I don't need to fight to be heard by a friend or even my wife. When I relax in His provision of care I can relax in any conversation because what they want to give to me is icing on the cake rather than a main entrée. *My relationship with God is the main course, and relationships with persons created in His image are dessert.*

To Women:

What your husband does for you is something you can give in return. His loving listening might indeed soften your heart, and make you want to listen to him in a similar way. In fact, it is a great strategy to get to know your husband in ways you have hoped to but haven't known how to. Lots of guys complain to us that their wives sure know how to talk, but not how to listen very well. *"I try to tell her things, but she just takes off on what she thinks and how she feels, so I think, 'Why try to tell her?'"* In our experience most guys aren't so tough, reluctant and out of touch with their feelings that they won't share them. They simply need a disciplined listener willing to share the airtime of their conversations to be willing to open their hearts.

Ladies, is this convicting? Or perhaps it's reassuring because you do this fairly well? But some of you might feel hopeless to get your husband to open up to you. Perhaps you've told yourself, *He's out of touch with his feelings,* or *He's not a talker.* Maybe both are true to an extent, but we've seen enough growth in couples that were stuck in boring and minimal conversational sharing that we don't accept these hopeless descriptions. Yes, it may take time to have the type of reciprocity in sharing that you would like to, but worthwhile accomplishments often take time and hard work. You can begin today by hanging on your husband's every word the next time he opens up about anything to you. He might share about work, a friend, or a hobby, but whatever it is—go with it! Listen well from a caring heart. Show him that whatever he brings out is worth your time and attention, and he just might share a bit more about other things.

To Men and Women:

If your loved ones, friends and co-workers were injected with truth serum, what would they say about you? Are you a *Holding Heart* who holds other's hearts as a sacred privilege? Are you a safe person with whom others will share their most intimate thoughts, feelings and desires?

How do the people you live with feel about you? To what degree do they share their honest thoughts and feelings without fear of rejection, judgment, invalidation or betrayal? On the other hand, are others genuinely interested in you and willing to set themselves aside to honor your heart? To what degree are you comfortable revealing your honest thoughts, feelings and desires with your closest family and friends? Who do you consider to be a Holding Heart in your life?

The bad news about effective listening and the major reason that it is so difficult is because it isn't human nature to hold other's hearts and the skill of doing it effectively isn't common. *The good news is that it is possible to develop a holding heart and the skills needed to convey compassion and love.*

Making it Work

Here's a real example of me sharing about a low time in our marriage with Jill. In the next section we lay out the steps for you to try it yourselves.

"Jeff, I heard you say that one of the saddest parts of my mom's death was the toll it took on me?" Jill said.

"That's right, honey. You were trying to be a good wife, a good mom and good daughter all at the same time, and there wasn't enough of you to go around, and not enough time in the day for you to do each role as well as you wanted. Not only were you losing someone you loved, but it seemed that you were also missing out on closeness with me and the kids because you tended so well to your mom for such long hours," I said.

"I hear that you felt sad for several reasons; losing my mom who really loved you, and seeing me in pain because my mom was in pain, but mostly that you felt sad for me because I was sad all around; sad about my mom, and sad about not being able to do well by my other closest relationships. Is that it?" Jill asked.

"It is. Although I didn't say some of it, I know you know some from other conversations, so it makes me feel like you are really trying to understand since you reached a little further than what I said just now," I finished.

The conversation was much longer, but you get the point. Jill was listening to me, not talking about her own memories and feelings. She focused on hearing what I said, not what she thought or felt. I could tell that she was focusing on trying to understand me because she reflected what she heard. That's the place to start, and it's often enough to keep the speaker going.

It worked for me. The more she listened, the more I shared, and the more I shared the more I heard myself talk the more I understood my thoughts and feelings, and the more she seemed to also. This is important because it's imperative to proactively strengthen a relationship and to keep it pleasurable. When I feel cared about and when I'm heard well, I feel loved. And when my tank is full of love I want to give back what I've received. That fills her tank, and the cycle of giving to each other continues.

The Skill of Effective Listening

Effective listening is also known as active listening, reflective listening, empathic listening, or mirroring. We also like to call it *loving listening* to remind ourselves and others to listen with a loving heart.

The basic skill calls for a listener to tell a speaker what they heard, in their own words. After hearing the listener's summary, the speaker either affirms that the listener understood by saying something like, *"Yes, you got it!"* or they graciously share again to give the listener another opportunity to understand.

While the skill of effective listening is relatively simple, doing it well requires tremendous discipline and effort. Yet, once basic principles are understood and practiced, it becomes a habit.

An often overlooked component of clear communication is the attitude of the speaker. *When you are given the opportunity to speak and you are gracious in response to inaccurate listening it takes pressure off the listener.* We have seen and experienced this done well by responses such as these:

- "That's some of what I wanted you to hear.
  Could I try again?"
- "That's not quite what I wanted you to hear.
  Perhaps I was unclear."
- "I think I was unclear. That's not quite what
  I'm trying to get at."

Contrast how you think you would feel in response to the first three bulleted responses as compared to these:

- "That's not what I said!"
- "You're not listening to me!"
- "Why can't you ever get what I mean?"

The point is that loving listening is an artful combination of heart and skill that requires persistent give and take between partners in marriage. In this respect, loving listening is best done as a dance that couples do in rhythm to the music of grace flowing from both of their hearts with notes of humility and selflessness as expressions of love.

Guidelines for Effective Listening

The skill of effective listening is based on a few guidelines that enhance the accuracy and flow of sharing between partners:

1. *The person speaking shares thoughts, feelings, and desires in segments of about three to five sentences.* More than that is hard for the listener to understand accurately, especially if what you are sharing is complex or evokes emotions in them. (A tip is to pretend that you are speaking through a translator. For a translator to keep up with your train of thought and interpret you accurately you would only speak in chunks of three-five sentences.)

   A. **If the speaker doesn't stop after three to five sentences, the listener can politely ask them to stop so they can summarize what they have just heard** — *"Can I interrupt you to make sure that I'm getting everything you are saying?"*

   B. **If the listener doesn't reflect back what they heard after the speaker shares, the speaker can ask the listener to reflect to them** — *"Would you mind reflecting what you heard me say? I'm not sure that I'm being clear and I want to make sure that we are communicating clearly."*

2. *The speaker either affirms the accuracy of what the listener heard, or tells the listener that they wanted them to hear something additional or different* — *"That's not quite what I wanted you to hear. Maybe I'm not being very clear. Would you mind if I tried again?"*

   A. **It is essential that the speaker affirms the listener's efforts** — *"Thanks for trying to hear me."* Remember, good-hearted effort counts for a lot! Effort to hear from one's heart can build a lot of positive equity into a relationship.

B. It is also extremely important for the speaker to take responsibility for their part of any unclear communications, instead of railing at the listener for "not listening".

    a. Destructive blaming statements include the following (positive alternatives are in parentheses):

- *"You didn't hear me!"* (*"I don't think I'm being clear"*).
- *"That's not what I said"* (*"Could I try again? That's not what I wanted you to hear"*).

3. *The speaker clarifies/repeats what they wanted to be understood by the listener.*

4. *The listener goes back to step #2.*

Perhaps listening to a conversation between Jill and me will help to illustrate these steps:

Jill: *"I hear you saying that you are disappointed by how things went between us last night after supper?"* (The context was that our shared plan for a quiet conversation under the stars didn't happen. I brought up how I was disappointed. Jill's reflection sounded sincere, so I was willing to share more.)

Jeff: *"Yes. I'd been looking forward to some relaxed time alone with you after our full day of activities. So when you started doing yet one more task I interpreted that you didn't care about us having some time alone."*

Jill: *"I hear that you'd been looking forward to some focused time for just us and that when I went to our home office to do one more task it said to you that I cared more about my task list than our relationship."*

Jeff: *"Yes. That's the way it seemed to me. I don't know how to understand what you really want when it looks like your words and actions are going in different directions."*

Jill: *"I hear you saying that you get confused because what I say and what I do look different to you."*

Jeff: *"Yes. Thanks for hearing me, honey. I'd like to hear your thoughts and feelings about this. Would you like to share now?"*

Jill shared and I listened. Eventually we hugged and prayed. Prolonged painful conflict had been avoided by respectful listening to each other's hearts from our hearts. And it all started with a simple reflection of something I said. That was a selfless act on Jill's part because she just as easily could have explained or defended her actions.

Consider how many wrong turns we could have made if one of us didn't take the initiative to listen:

- If Jill had shared her feelings before hearing mine, *"You were frustrated! I was frustrated!"*
- If she would have minimized my feelings, *"Oh come on. We've had lots of time together alone recently. Is it really that big of a deal?"*
- If she would have focused on a part of my message or changed the focus from my feelings to hers, *"You knew I had to get that task done before I could relax. By the way, did I tell you…?"*

Jill and I have seen many couples extract themselves from dark and painful places by simply listening to each other with heart and skill.[49] Some couples have seen a lot of turbulent water go under the bridge of their relationship. Many have pent up resentments, hurts and fears about sharing honestly with each other. Nevertheless, the heart and skill of loving listening can be exceptionally effective with such challenging content. It's not easy, but it's definitely worthwhile because when couples achieve even minimum levels of ability to effectively listen to each other, they are well on their way to building and sustaining a marriage to be excited about.

Some people complain that reflecting what they hear in a conversation back to their partner feels robotic and unnatural. If that's the way it feels to you, here are a few tips that may help you to relax as you listen and practice effective listening skills.

- *Reflect in your own words* vs. parroting verbatim. This will remove the feeling that you are being robotic and unnatural.
- *Be brief* in order to keep the focus on the speaker.
- *Be tentative* vs. sure. For example, *"I think what I'm hearing you say is…"* vs. *"What you said is…"*

When Jill and I reflect to each other and to clients our average reflection is one or two sentences that goes something like this, *"What I hear you saying is?"* said with a bit of a questioning tone in our voice that says, *"Is that right? Is that what you want me to hear?"* or *"I think you're saying)?"* or *"So, I think I hear you saying…"* The point is that the listener listens from a posture of humility with no prior assumption about what the speaker means, thus the question, *"Am I hearing what you want me to hear?"*

Overall, reflections are received much better when spoken in tones of humility without any hint of arrogance. For comparison, listen for arrogance and impatience expressed in the following phrases: *"I already know that"* or *"You already said that."* The result of such unkind and impatient responses (and sometimes the interruption of the speaker) can shut the other person down. When it happens to me I think, *Why would I keep trying to share with you when you assume that you already know all the answers and don't care to hear what I have to say?*

Troubleshooting Tips

1. Disagreements and Emotional Triggers

As simple as effective listening appears to be, it isn't easy and there are multitudes of ways it can go awry. For instance, conversations about conflicted and emotional topics can break down because our partner strongly disagrees with something we said and/or it triggers some strong emotions for them. What then? Too often the triggered partner hijacks the conversation by making a comment, sharing an opinion, or moving on to another related topic. When this shift takes place, a heart holding opportunity is lost, at least temporarily.

Such conversations can be recovered with a 'do over'. This requires grace from the speaker, and willingness from the listener to regroup and refocus. It can go something like this:

Speaker: *"I'm not feeling heard. You started talking about some-thing else rather than reflecting what I shared."*
Listener: *"I'm sorry. Could we try again?"*
Speaker: *"Sure. Thank you."*

Remember that even when emotions arise due to the content, or when the speaker becomes offended by poor listening that a return to a commitment to hold each other's hearts with listening is an effective way to arrest difficult conversations before they unravel. Try it to see how far it can take you in working through emotionally charged and difficult conversations.

2. Tips for Listeners:

A. As a listener it is important to set aside your reactions and responses in order to listen effectively. This is a significant gift you can give to your partner over and over. *Note:* Some listeners struggle to reflect thoughts and feelings with which they disagree. Remember, as the listener you aren't necessarily agreeing with the speaker. You are simply honoring their perspective and saying that you care and respect them enough to work hard to carefully hear their perspective. You might have a radically different viewpoint and have feelings that are entirely different from the other person, but the fact remains that you can do an awesome job of reflecting.

B. Trust God to honor the fact that you are setting yourself aside in listening. The result will often be that the speaker will want to hear your heart, and will give to you as you gave to them.

C. Remember, it's not "right reflections" we're after but "effective reflections". There isn't only one perfect reflection. Different listeners will reflect differently and still be equally effective.

3. **Tips for Speakers:**
   A. Listeners struggle to remember what was said if the speaker says more than five sentences. Speakers, be nice to your listeners. Give them frequent opportunities to reflect what they heard (about every three-five sentences).

   B. Be liberal with praise for efforts to listen well. Even if your listener didn't hear what you wanted them to hear, thank them for trying and give them grace to try again. Good listening is hard work, and praise provides needed encouragement to continue trying.

4. **When all else fails...reflect what you heard**
   Effective listening is the first and most important skill you need to coach your own marriage, and it is useful in all other relationships. In fact, when you are lost in any conversation, unsure of what to say or do next, simply reflect the last thing you heard the speaker say. I'll reinforce this by sharing one of my most embarrassing moments.

   I fell asleep during one of the first counseling sessions I provided during graduate school. I was in training, and Jill and I were living a typical post graduate lifestyle. I'd been up late working second shift at a hospital to make ends meet, and then got up early for an eight a.m. counseling session. It was one of those, "Where's the coffee" mornings. Unfortunately, my client spoke in a soft monotone. He might as well have been a sleep machine that makes soothing sounds because that's the effect he had on me. I awoke with a start in the middle of one of his sentences, not knowing how long I'd been unconscious. Oh no! What to do? Thankfully he said a bit more before pausing. I reached for the only skill that could save me; effective listening. I summarized the last part of his sentence. He nodded and continued. Rookie counselor saved by effective listening!

Likewise, in your marriage conversations, reflecting what you heard your partner say is never the wrong thing to do. It is a gesture of good-will toward the relationship and an effective strategy to convey that you care about their thoughts, feelings and desires... but only if you do it with heart; thus the importance of the concept of Holding Hearts.

The Role of Effective Listening in Coaching Your Marriage

Question: How do you know when to prescribe effective listening for your marriage?

Answer: All the time; there's never a bad time or situation for listening!

Listen with heart and skill when:
- *Your spouse says:*
  - "Can I talk to you for a minute?"
  - "I really want you to hear me about this."
  - "I don't feel like you're getting what I'm saying."

- *When you:*
  - Want to build equity in your marriage by making a positive deposit.
  - Want to love your partner without touching them.

- Want to reconnect after a brief or lengthy separation (workday, travel apart, etc.).
- ***When the marriage:***
  - Is feeling strained or stressed.
  - Has been conflicted for any reason.
  - Needs one of you to be the first one to take a step toward the marriage.

When else do you think you would coach your marriage to listen with heart and skill? Seriously! Don't wait for us to prescribe the right time. That's the point of you becoming savvy in your discernment about what your marriage needs and when. *This book won't accomplish its purpose unless you become active and creative problem-solvers that take what you've learned and apply it where you need it and ONLY YOU know that!*

One of the best outcomes of you learning to coach your own marriage is the confidence you will have to take a step back at any point in your married life to ask what your marriage needs to get back on track, to have more pleasure, to be healthier, etc. As you habitually listen to each other from your hearts (as you hold each other's hearts), you will have plenty of ideas about how it would be good for your marriage to grow and change. So listen with heart every time you have the chance.

If your partner isn't on board with the idea of coaching your marriage, take hope in the fact that sometimes it takes just one of you to change for the other to change. Effective listening is something anyone can decide to do without getting the consent of the person that you are listening to. *If you are the only one that wants to work on your marriage you can still do your part to listen effectively.*

To do this, make sure to prepare your heart. The listening prayer is a good way to do this. Ask God's help to set yourself aside, to ignore triggers, and to accurately hear and reflect what your partner tries to communicate with you. Stay committed to this, especially if the conversation gets rough. Sometimes in relationships where resentments have been built up it can take considerable time and effort to continue listening through a barrage of pent up thoughts and frustrations, but once cleansed, the partner that has spoken their honest feelings will often express gratitude and relief. We often see previously unwilling partners recognize and appreciate being listened to with love. So, if you are stymied in your relationship, know that listening to your unwilling and unmotivated partner might be a first step to nurture them toward willingness to listen to you and to coach your marriage together.

When you aren't sure what to do in conversation, ask a question around a topic that you are curious about and then listen. Keep telling your partner what you heard them say. Don't worry if you feel awkward at first. That will pass as you become comfortable telling your partner what you heard. What usually happens is that you will get so lost in what your partner is saying that you will forget to be self-conscious about how you are doing the skill. Plus, from the speaker's point of view, being listened to is so refreshing that the last thing they notice is any awkwardness in your manner.

The following is a typical conversation we have with couples after a few sessions of Marriage Coaching or their first class in Marriage Coaching training.[50] It illustrates the power of simple effective listening from the heart.

"What's better since our last session?" is often one of the first questions we ask a couple at the beginning of a Marriage Coaching session.

"Well, we had a great conversation the other night. Bob shared some things with me at a level that he's never really gone to before," Karen said.

"How did that happen, Bob?" we asked.

"I felt comfortable sharing because Karen seemed to care about what I thought and how I felt about a situation at work that's been really stressful for me. She simply listened and every so often told me what she was hearing, and so I just kept going," Bob said.

"How was this conversation different than others? What did each of you do more or less as compared to other conversations?" we asked.

"Well, I know I've not been a very good listener sometimes," said Karen. *"I know that Bob has tried to tell me things, but I've either told him what I think or how I would feel in that situation, or let it trigger things that I want to tell him. This time something clicked. I realized as he began to share some thoughts and feelings about recent challenges with his boss that it was a golden opportunity to hold his heart in my hands! Bob was literally reaching down inside to some tender feelings to share with me. That was one of my original complaints when we started coaching, remember? I wanted him to be more open with me and talk to me more. Well, listening like this really works!"* Karen exclaimed.

"Bob, do you have anything to add?" we asked.

"Just that it does work. I really appreciated how Karen focused on what I was sharing. She seemed to have all the time in the world, and that made me feel like what I was saying was more important than anything else. I could tell she was trying because she made efforts to say back to me in her own words what she thought I was trying to say. She didn't get it all the first time, but because she was trying so hard and seemed to care I found myself willing to clarify and repeat a few times. You know, simply listening to each other like this could revolutionize our marriage!"

"Yes it can!" Jill and I happily declared with knowing smiles.

The bad news is that effective listening is difficult and that many people don't do it very well. The good news is that it can be learned through practice by anyone. So, take heart, and grow from the place you are to the place you want to be and need to be!

If you don't get anything else from this book, get this—***Effective*** *listening from the heart is an essential part of the foundation of your marriage!* In fact, we believe that the quality, depth and fulfillment of our relationships is directly proportional to the quality of the combination of listening we do to *hold others hearts*!

CHAPTER SIX
Reflection Questions:

1. How do you rate yourself as a listener on a scale of 1-10? If you answer a one or higher but less than 10 then there is something positive to build on!

_____

_____

_____

_____

_____

2. How do you think improvements in effective listening could benefit your marriage?

_____

_____

_____

_____

_____

3. What motivates you to improve your listening? How can you stay motivated to listen to your partner's heart even when it feels like they're not listening very well to you?

_____

_____

_____

_____

_____

The Heart & Skill of Effective Asking

In the last chapter we learned how to hold our partner's heart through effective listening. Just as an obstetrician needs to know how to catch a baby before they deliver it, we need to know how to hold our partner's heart before we even attempt to open it.

Since we now know how to hold a heart, we can now learn how to open a heart through effective questions. Effective questions are levers that gently invite our partner to share honest thoughts, feelings and desires.

What your partner shares will either trickle or pour out, based on a number of factors including mood, personality, their level of trust in you, the history of your conversations, the level of your skill, the goodness of your heart, etc. If you are thinking, *They won't talk to me very much*, or *Our conversations aren't very open*, we want to encourage you. We've seen this change fairly rapidly when effective questions are asked from a posture of sincerity and compassion, and when one's curious asking is followed by careful and loving listening.

Here is the simple formula we use for life-giving conversations:

> *Effective Asking* + *Effective Listening* = *Life-giving Conversations*
> *(that opens the heart)*   *(that holds the heart)*

The Heart of Asking

The simple agenda Jill and I have when we meet with a couple is to hear, see and feel their thoughts, feelings, and desires concerning their marriage: the client.[51] Asking and listening accomplishes this objective, and it is something you can do for your marriage just like Jill and I do for ours. We ask each other open questions about each of these components, and then reflect what we hear each other say.

Asking invites sharing. When it is done from a posture of sincere curiosity and it is accompanied by effective listening, the probability is high that your spouse will share their honest thoughts, feelings, and desires. Again, asking isn't just a skill. *It is the yearning of a caring and compassionate heart to understand.*

The effective asker doesn't simply want information. They want to grasp what life looks like and feels like to their partner. They want to know the desires of their partner's heart so that they can help to fulfill them. They want to understand because they ache to draw close, and the only way to get that close is to draw out and hold their partner's heart. Effective asking opens the heart so it can be seen, heard, felt, and held.

We think that asking to discover what life looks like and feels like is a Christ-like behavior. Throughout his life, Jesus looked on people with compassion.[52] Compassion is defined as, *"sympathetic consciousness of others distress combined with a desire to alleviate it".*[53] Consider many of Jesus' words and actions including numerous healings and His weeping in response to a friend's death.[54]

Thus, being curious about the reality of others; their thoughts, feelings and desires is a loving, compassionate behavior that you express when you ask from your heart what they think, how they feel and what they want. This process has the potential to make any conversation a life-giving and transformational conversation.

The Skill of Asking: What to Ask About

As we mentioned earlier, thoughts, feelings and desires are three areas to explore in intimate conversations. What does your partner think, how do they feel and what do they want?

Now, let's look at some possible questions in each of those three categories.

1. Thoughts
   "What have you been thinking about?"

This question is a highly effective conversation-starter. It gives the speaker a choice about what to share, just like the famous projective question, *"Look at the clouds and tell me what you see?"* It gives a person freedom to share whatever is on their mind, and gives you an inroad to potential concerns and desires. I use it with Jill and our children to get a bearing on what matters to them at the moment; what they are hoping for, what they might be anxious about or things they want to get done. Here are some other specific examples:

- "What thoughts did you have about our marriage when you decided to call for a coaching appointment?"
- "What thoughts have you been having about our marriage?"
- "What do you think it will take to accomplish your goals in our marriage?"
- "What is it that you can't stop thinking about this week?"

2. Feelings
"What are some of the biggest feelings you've experienced lately?"

It is impossible to have life experiences or to think thoughts without accompanying feelings. If you know what a person has been thinking about or experiencing in their life circumstances you can query their emotions about it. From our experience as counselors and coaches, this is the area that many people aren't sure about and need to be asked about. Here are some example questions:

- "How were you feeling about our marriage when you decided to call for coaching?"
- "What has been the biggest feeling you've had recently about our marriage?"
- "What feeling(s) would you like to have about our marriage?"
- "When you cry about our marriage what feelings are you having?"

3. **Desires**
   "What do you want?"

Desires are the bridge from awareness to action. When you understand what you want, you can focus your energy and efforts towards your desired goal. When you are not clear on what you want, you will likely wander aimlessly around not knowing where you are going. Once you have explored thoughts and feelings it is natural to explore desires. You can do this with your spouse, or by yourself. Here are some example questions (change the form depending on whether you are asking yourself, asking your partner, or asking your marriage). When you ask yourself or your partner these questions you will elicit your desires and your spouse's desires, but remember, there is another entity to ask when you are attempting to coach your own marriage. Your marriage must be asked these questions too:

- "How would I/you/our marriage like things in our marriage to be?"
- "What would I/you/our marriage like to start or stop happening, or to happen more or less in our marriage?"
- "What would I/you/our marriage like in regard to communication and conflict resolution in our marriage?"
- "What one thing do I/you want from your spouse more than anything else?"
- "What do I/you want others to be able to say about your marriage?"
- "When we look back on this season of growth in our marriage, what do I want to hear from God about how I engaged this season of our relationship?"

Thoughts, Feelings and Desires
Most of us are oriented around one of these components more than the others. Listen to anyone long enough and you'll pick up whether

they think more thoughts or feel more feelings. Our suggestion for complete conversations is that you seek to round out your understanding by asking about the parts you don't hear.

When a person primarily shares their thoughts, make sure to ask about their feelings, and when they primarily share their feelings, go for their thoughts. Most people lean to one side or the other. We need understanding of both for a complete picture and full perspective.

For example, if you are curious about some of the desires your partner shared, learn more by asking open questions that focus on the following: how, what, when and where. For instance, if they said, *"I want a vacation,"* you could say, *"I'm curious to hear more about what you **want** for a vacation?"* or, *"**When** would you like to take a vacation?"* *"**Where** would you like to take a vacation?"* *"**How** long would you like a vacation to be?"*

Here's a table to give you a visual of the possible combinations of interrogatives and areas to ask about:

	How	What	When	Where
Thoughts				
Feelings				
Desires				

Remember, the process of asking and listening builds the relationship because you are sharing your honest thoughts and feelings with each other. And, the practical value is that your partner is putting you in a position to meet the desires of their heart. This is exactly how seeds got planted into my mind to surprise Jill with a birthday trip to a specific beach setting a few years ago! On several occasions when questioning her about her desires for a vacation, I asked what she wanted. She said how much she wanted to go back to Anna Maria Island because it was one of the best vacations we'd had in the past. While we were sitting together on the beach it was fun to think back on the conversations that revealed her heart to me in a way that I wanted to fulfill!

You can construct effective questions by being curious about what your partner thinks, feels and wants. The easiest way to come up with them is to ask yourself questions about your partner.

- I wonder what they think about_____ ?
- I wonder how they feel about _____ ?
- I wonder what they would like in regard to _____ ?

The simple transition to an effective question for our spouse is the way the words are arranged:

- What do you think about_____ ?
- How do you feel about _____ ?
- What would you like in regard to _____ ?

Simply ask yourself what you would like to know about your spouse; what their perspective is on a situation, how they felt about a recent event, or what they want in regard to something planned in the future. Next, turn it into a question by asking how, when, what or where. There, [now] you have a potentially effective question.

Putting it All Together

Life-giving conversations happen when we ask about other's thoughts, feelings or desires, they share with us, and we listen and reflect from the heart. The process is as follows:

1. Ask

It is easy to get the conversational ball rolling by simply asking an open question (see Asking Rule Two below) about your partner's thoughts, feelings or desires.

- What do you think about_____ ?
- How do you feel about _____ ?
- What would you like in regard to _____ ?

If you want to take this a step further, go back to the asking Table, What, When, Where, How about thoughts, feelings and desires. See how many questions you can come up with for each box. Then imagine what your partner might say in response to your questions. This might help you to decide which questions you want to ask.

What makes a good question?
- It makes you think.
- It is expressed in a way that demonstrates sincere interest.
- It opens your heart. You find yourself wanting to answer and glad you were asked.
- It is relevant to what a person knows about what matters to you.

2. Listen

When it is your turn to listen, simply listen. Try to remember that your partner is opening the door of desires in their heart. Some couples like to take notes. We recommend this to help you remember. One wife said, *"You can't imagine what it meant to me that he took notes. It said that he really cared and that he wanted to meet my needs! Suddenly I started noticing things around the house getting done by his initiative from just one simple conversation!"*

3. Reflect

Reflect back to your partner what you hear them telling you.

To help you further develop the heart and skill of asking we have created a few asking rules that will assist you in coaching your marriage.

Asking Rule One: Ask, Don't Tell

Because we are ultimately pursuing growth and change in our marriage and because motivation is more important than information in the change process, it is imperative that we ask instead of tell when we want to have life-giving conversations. In coaching we say, *"Ask don't tell."*

When you are attempting to have a life-giving conversation with your spouse or another individual, avoid giving advice. This is especially important when they are facing a challenge or wanting to resolve a problem. Why are they sharing it with you? Do they want your ideas? If they do it is certainly appropriate to say what you think. But how many times have you given unsolicited advice without them asking, or prematurely given advice that resulted in them being upset because they "just wanted you to listen"?

At the time of this writing Jill is attempting to negotiate a pay raise for a promotion in some work outside of our ministry. I have strong ideas about what she needs to do to accomplish the raise, but she has been clear that she wants to learn and grow by negotiating this herself. That's a clear message to me to ask instead of telling. As we talk about this subject I have been listening, reflecting what I hear, and asking her what she thinks, how she feels and what she wants. The effect is that she is staying open, and willing to share with me. My listening and asking is helpful to her evaluation of options she is considering.

Is your spouse negotiating something challenging at work or in an extended family relationship? Are you tempted to tell them what they should do? Pause to think about what it says to a person when you give unsolicited advice:

- That you are smarter than them.
- That they don't know what to do and won't be able to figure it out.
- That the way they approach problems isn't adequate.

Compare your answers to the results of asking instead of telling:

- That you are curious about what they think, how they feel and what they want.
- That you respect their ability to think through challenges for themselves.
- That you trust their judgment and are willing to bless them to act accordingly.

Asking Rule Two: Use the Right Kind of Question

Since effective questions are levers that open couple's hearts it is essential to ask the types of questions that lead them to freely share their honest thoughts, feelings and desires, and to avoid the kinds of questions that could be counterproductive.

Now, let's look a little closer at types of questions. There are two kinds of questions that we suggest avoiding when you are trying to open your partner's heart to share with you, and one type to try to ask.

Open Questions – Open questions invite longer answers. They cannot be responded to with yes or no, and they don't offer solutions. They most often begin with, (What? How? When? Where?), and generally avoid 'Why'.

Examples:

- *"What have you found most interesting/helpful from this book so far?"*
- *"How do you think it could be helpful to us to do the exercises at the end of the chapters?"*
- *"How did you decide to buy and read this book? What do you want from it?"*

Closed Questions – These are easy to recognize, and they DO have a place, but not as often as most people use them. The usual result of a closed question is a yes or no answer. The asker doesn't really learn much from the response, and the speaker doesn't get much air-time to share before the conversational ball is passed back to the asker.

Examples:

- *"Do you like this book?"*
- *"Do you think we should do some of the exercises at the end of the chapters?"*
- *"Did you like the movie we just watched?"*

Better Questions:
- *"What do you like about this book?"*
- *"What are your thoughts about sharing our answers to the questions at the end of the chapters?"*
- *"What did you enjoy in the movie we just watched?"*

Do you see how the questions in the second set are better questions because they have potential to elicit longer and more informative answers?

Solution-focused Questions – These are tricky. While you think you are asking a good question, you are actually making a suggestion in the form of a question. (*"Have you thought about asking your mother in-law to call before coming over to your house?"*). You are actually telling the person: *"You should tell your mother in-law to call before coming over."* Solution-focused questions sound like questions, but they have a suggestion embedded in them.

Examples:
- *"Don't you think this book is absolutely wonderful?"*
- *"Don't you agree that it's a waste of time to do exercises at the end of the chapters?"*
- *"Wasn't that the best movie you've ever seen?"*

Hopefully you now see why open questions are the best. Here are some open questions that you might be asked in a Marriage Coaching session with Jill and me. Note, as open questions they cannot be answered with a simple yes or no answer. They require an explanation.

Warm up Questions:
- *"How did you and your spouse meet?"*
- *"What attracted you to him/her?"*
- *"How did you decide to get married?"*
- *"When were you happiest and most excited about your marriage?"*
- *"When were you at your lowest point?"*

Questions to Evaluate a Marriage

- *"Where are you now in terms of pleasure and satisfaction in your relationship?" (On a scale of 1-10?)*
- *"How did you get to that point? "*
- *"Where would you like to be?*

Notice that between the two sets of questions that we also used all four of the different interrogatives: how, what, when and where. But we didn't use why. Why is a tricky word that can elicit defensiveness from the person being questioned because it can communicate judgment. "Why did you do that?" is sometimes heard as "That was stupid. How did you ever come up with such a dumb idea?" Try this instead, "How did you decide to do that?" Still, your attitude behind the question will make a difference. Are you truly curious about how they made that decision? And are you willing to be respectful to them for the rationale they present?

Asking Rule Three: Allow Your Questions to Percolate Naturally From Your Heart

Are you a naturally curious person? Does the way other people think about things intrigue you? Do you ever wonder, *"What's it like to be them? How does life look and feel to them?"*

Our oldest daughter, Carly is naturally curious. When driving through the city she wonders, "What is that man thinking about? What does he care about? How is he feeling about his life right now?" This is exactly the process that births effective questions; wondering what is in other's hearts.

You might be tempted to try to memorize specific questions. That's fine. There are some great stock questions that will start great conversations, but don't limit yourself to questions that you've memorized. Even Jill and I have a list of favorite questions and we continue to make additions to the list.[55] It's just that we don't want you to miss the art of forming and asking effective questions as a dynamic Holy Spirit guided process. In this way, the art of asking effective questions to open your partner's heart is not something that can be planned in advance like a structured interview that follows a script. Rather, it is an art form that requires faith that God will present questions to ask during conversations.

Don't get stuck trying to ask the "right" question. What we've found is that it is more helpful to think about all of the possible effective questions. Effective questions are the ones that your partner responds to by sharing their thoughts, feelings and desires. These questions percolate to the surface of your mind during a conversation, and they are shaped by unceasing prayer as you ask and listen. In Jill and my conversations I often pray silently: *Lord, I really want to understand what this looks like and feels like to Jill. Please help me to get it, and please give me insight and understanding as she shares.*

Many couples we train and coach are surprised by the direction of conversations and the questions that arise as they follow one topic to another.[56] One question leads to another, and as we share with each other more questions arise that we couldn't have thought of or scripted in advance. While this might be uncomfortable for those of us that like to have things specifically planned in advance, the organic nature of life-giving conversations simply doesn't allow it.

While coaching couples, Jill and I freely ask questions that come to our minds because we trust that the Holy Spirit has been putting them together. Internally, our self-talk goes like this: *I wonder what they thought about that experience. I wonder how they felt when that happened. I wonder what he/she wants.* These musings turn into open questions that we ask couples as simply and succinctly as possible.

If you are new at this it is easy to get stuck trying to ask the perfect question. As I began with my first counseling clients in 1988, I had a recurring dream about a session with the same client. They said something, and I didn't know what to say, so I clicked my pen which froze them in time (Great pen! I'll bet some of you would love to have one to freeze some people in your life!). In the dream my client literally froze. They didn't move, speak, or think. While they were frozen I pulled out all my books to search for the next right question to ask. Can you identify with this?

Today, in my marriage (as well as in coaching and counseling sessions), I know that the right question is the question that God brings to my mind in response to what it looks like and feels like to be Jill. I also know that a question was the right question when she responds by sharing her heart. The right question is the question that your spouse is not only willing to answer, but wants to answer. The right question is the question that tells you something fresh and something deeper about your spouse's honest thoughts, feelings or desires. There is no single right question but a multitude of effective questions as evidenced by your partner's response.

Right questions are effective questions; questions that your spouse responds to by sharing their heart.

Asking Rule Four: Following your Intuition

Open questions are developed from a combination of intuition and curiosity. Sometimes we suspect that our partner has important ideas, feelings and desires about something in particular. Usually we get those ideas when we've picked up on some kind of indicator that triggers our curiosity. In coaching lingo we call these *intuition indicators*. These are like yellow or red flags in a conversation; things that are said or the way they're said that alerts us to the importance of what our partner is sharing and give us a clue about where to ask additional questions.

It is good practice to note these, and to consider asking about them. When in doubt about what to ask, it is rarely wrong or ineffective to say, *"I heard you say _____, which made me curious, and sounds important to you. Would you share more?"*

Key indicators are strong emotion, a person's own discernment, and transition points. Be careful to avoid diagnosing. Here are some samples to help make this clear.

- *Strong emotion* – Voice tone and/or volume, tears, facial expression, etc. *"If she cared she would listen when I try to tell her*

*what I want different, but she just interrupts to say I don't have
a right to feel that way" (said with a tone of anger).*

- *A person's own discernment* – The speaker offers their understanding of something about themselves, their partner or the
relationship. *"I have noticed that when she yells at me about
my driving that I drive that much more aggressively. I think it
is because her yelling makes me mad and nervous."*

- *Transition points* – The speaker says something to indicate
that an event was a really important time (positive or negative)
for their relationship. *"It was when he went to Iraq for his first
deployment four years ago that things really got hard for us."*

Practice forming a curious question that you might ask in response
to each of the intuition indicator examples above. If you get stuck, go
back to the table under the paragraph, 'Thoughts, Feelings and Desires'
and the table with the interrogatives *how, what, when and where*. Then
check out our examples below.

If we heard the statements above in a coaching session we would reflect what we heard and then listen if they wanted to say more. We might
also ask questions such as these (based on the examples above):

- *"How do her interruptions affect you?"*
- *"What would you like different from her?"*
- *"How did things get really hard in your marriage when he
went to Iraq?"*

Do you see how simple and brief an effective question can be?

Asking Rule Five: Don't be Afraid of Silence

Professional coaches are trained that silence in response to their
questions is not a sign of a bad question but rather a GREAT question.
Why? Because great questions help people to think! If you ask your

partner a question and they don't answer right away, don't take it as unwillingness. Remember, most people ask closed questions that require only a yes or no answer. But an open question requires some thought, and a more detailed response.

Sometimes your partner may comment on your question before answering, *"That's a really good question. I need some time to think about that."* Great! Don't be disappointed. Communication is an ongoing process not a one-time event. They will probably come back to you to share their response after processing for a while. Be prepared to be patient and celebrate these hiatuses in conversation. They are likely to move your spouse to a deeper level of self-awareness and will take your relationship to a more intimate place.

All conversations have ebb and flow. Some of your questions will be responded to quickly and others will take time to answer. As your spouse winds down what they want to share in response to your questions, ask again as other questions percolate to the surface. One question leads to another. It is rare to be able to script an entire conversation from the start to finish. Rather, it is more likely that you will be led from one question to another per your partner's answers. Relax as you enjoy a journey into the depths of the soul of the one you love and enjoy the closeness that results.

A great way to become comfortable with the time and effort required to respond to powerful questions is to be coached. While this book has been written to stand alone to help you to develop the ability to ask and to listen effectively, we would be remiss to not point out how much can be learned about the process of coaching by being coached. The obvious difference between learning by reading and by being coached is that when you are coached live, you will be asked more questions that are specific to your circumstances. Plus, being coached by a great Marriage Coaching couple is a great way to become a great Marriage Coaching couple. As one of our former clients says, *"Being coached lets you look behind the curtain to see what the wizard is doing."*[57]

When I am being coached, I don't notice periods of silence. In fact, I appreciate the silence so I can think about the questions I'm being asked. Experiencing the value of silence combined with my patience from those who coach me has helped me to learn to be patient when Jill and I coach our own marriage. In fact, it isn't uncommon for one of us to say in response to questions, *"I need to think about that."* When Jill says she needs some time to think I know she will come back to that topic in our next conversation. Often she initiates conversations by saying, *"I've been thinking about what you asked me..."*

Speaking of thinking, I want to say a word about different processing styles. Introverts (those that rejuvenate better in silence and solitude) need quiet time to think about questions, while extroverts (those that get energy from being with people) prefer to think out loud about questions. So, awareness of your style and your spouse's is helpful in order that you can honor each other's preferences.

As you learn the skill of asking and how to develop powerful questions, we want you to remember that ultimately the goal of asking is not to see how much you can ask, or for you to fill in every blank of your curiosity. The goal of asking is to make clear to your partner that you want to understand, appreciate, and respect their heart; to draw closer through shared understanding. Effective questions will help you to accomplish this.

Asking Rule Six: Ask for what you Want!

"'I want to make love," I said. *"What do you want, Jill?"*

"I want to take a walk with you, and talk for a while, and then maybe make love," she said.

There. Our desires are on the table. Now, hopefully we can do something about helping each other to fulfill them. The alternative is to leave them unspoken. *Too often couples leave their desires hidden.* That can hurt and lead to resentment, especially when one partner doesn't notice or guess correctly about needs the other partner has but hasn't expressed. This sounds like a description of immaturity, we know, but without intentionality about using skills and exercises to communicate thoroughly and accurately, guesswork is what we're left with.

Ideally, in a mutually submitted relationship we will both seek to meet each other's needs. Just like Chip and Dale, the infamous cartoon chipmunks, it is possible to create a process of communicating about our wants that result in us almost tripping over each other to meet each other's needs. When this happens both partners often enjoy the feeling of love and pleasure on a regular basis.

Dr. Bill Harley[58] says that this is some of the best marriage insurance available; *being keenly aware of each other's needs and making consistent efforts to meet them.* But, how can we meet our partner's needs/desires if we don't know what they are? Here is a little exercise that Jill and I often do that elicits hopes and desires in a manner that is both fun and easy. We call it the Desires Exercise.[59] Here's an example of how to do it:

Jeff: *"Jill, what do you want?"*
Jill: *"I want_____. What do you want?"*
Jeff: *"I want_____. What do you want?"*

Repeat asking and answering until you run out of wants. Lest you think it's all about sex, here is another sample conversation:

Jeff: *"What do you want from today, Jill?"*
Jill: *"I want to get the living room painted and the garage door fixed. What do you want?"*
Jeff: *"I want a hamburger. I'm hungry. What do you want?"*
Jill: *"I want to go lay by the pool, but not long so I don't get burnt. What do you want?"*
Jeff: *"I want to watch the final round in the U.S. Open. What do you want?"*
Jill: *"I want to take Laura shopping so she can get some clothes for summer, and to get some charcoal so we can cook-out later. A hamburger sounds good to me, too!"*

Sharing wants doesn't have to be just about big things. Simply sharing our desires for the day gives us an opportunity to co-create a schedule to satisfy our mutual and different desires. Meeting such seemingly trivial needs can go a long way in building equity in a relationship.

We find it fun and healthy to serve each other's needs. It even seems biblical![60] When I take initiative to serve Jill, it increases the likelihood that she will serve me. This is a great way to create a positive economy of giving to each other in a way that is self-reinforcing. *How do you get what you want? Give your partner what they want.*

Now, how about that walk, honey?

Asking Rule Seven: Practice

And again, it takes practice. Just like riding a bike, the more you do it, the more proficient you become. The skill of asking can be practiced in any conversation, not just with your partner. Practice by asking curious questions when you talk with colleagues at work, friends at school, partners in ministry, etc.

Now, after you understand your partner's honest thoughts, feelings, and desires, and they understand yours, you are ready to honor the desires of each other's hearts by setting shared goals for your marriage. Remember, a coaching approach isn't just about exploration and discovery of what another person thinks, feels or wants, but also about setting and accomplishing goals based on desires and motivation.

Before we move on to how to set effective goals in chapter 8, take a few minutes to practice answering some open questions about your thoughts, feelings and desires in your marriage. This will not only deepen your understanding and appreciation for the effectiveness of these types of questions, but will also provide some content that you might want to use in the goal-setting step.

*This is a great place to pause reading to do an exercise to discover the desires of your heart and your partner's heart. (See Appendix C)

CHAPTER SEVEN
Reflection Questions:

1. Rate your ability to ask effective questions on a scale of 1-10. What is one thing you could do to raise your ability one or two points?

_____

_____

_____

_____

_____

2. What stands out to you about the heart of asking? How motivated are you to cultivate your heart with curious and unselfish compassion? Why?

_____

_____

_____

_____

_____

3. What are you most curious about regarding your spouse: what they think, how they feel, or what they want? What is one thing you feel curious about right now? Try formulating a question using one of the open interrogatives (what, where, when, how), and then make a time to ask them.

_____

_____

_____

_____

_____

Effective Goal-Setting

Coaching is an intentional conversation that has the objective of getting something done. It's not casual chatting. It's about taking action. *In coaching if you don't have an active goal that you are motivated to accomplish, then it's not coaching.* Since your marriage is the coaching client, then the goals you set are about taking action for the benefit of your marriage. This differs from individual coaching where only the individual sets the goal.

So, what do you do after you've asked some questions to open your partner's heart and you've used effective listening to hold it? What do you do with your understanding of what your partner wants and what your marriage needs? There are two choices. Sit on it or work on it.

Are you tired of only talking about change, saying, *"It's great that we talked about it? Now what are we going to **do** about it?"*

The way we see it, setting goals isn't optional in marriage because God is always engaging us to grow and change to become more and more the people He made us to be and to prepare us to do the things He made us to do.[61] Viewed like this, *setting goals is a responsive act of worship.* It is the consummation of transformational conversations with our spouses during which our hearts have been affected with understanding of what we each think, how we each feel and what we each want. In other words, setting and working on goals is love in action; love for our spouse[62] and love for God.

God Himself inspires us to reach for more of the pleasure and purpose that He has for us in our marriages and He both inspires and blesses action because it is the way He works to help us to do His will. Ultimately, we know that He wants us to experience pleasure (joy) in Him and each other, and to live purpose-focused lives as teams of two *for His Kingdom!*

Setting goals based on desires is a way to say, *Father, thank you for what you have given us. In faith we aspire for more and better. We recognize that you are constantly at work to give us opportunities to grow and change for your purposes and your Glory. In Jesus' name. Amen.*

A Covenant Approach to Goals for Your Marriage

The word covenant is more sacred than the word goal. And, it is used less frequently in everyday language. In addition, it indicates mutual responsibility for the parties in covenant.

In our marriage we understand our covenant as a sacred promise to persevere in our relationship for the purposes God has in mind for it. Thus, when we set shared goals in our marriage and for our marriage, we are fulfilling our promise to actively support and defend our covenant with God regarding our marriage. This makes the formation and pursuit of shared goals more important than personal fulfillment. As explained in previous paragraphs, a covenant commitment to attain a shared goal is an ongoing response of gratitude and servitude to the One who brought us together and sustains our marriage relationship as a team of two for the purpose of advancing His Kingdom.

Please keep this sacred purpose in mind and refer to the document "A Covenant for Our Shared Goal" in Appendix D) as you read and work through the remainder of this chapter.

From Desires to Action—A Step-wise process to setting goals for your marriage.

Dreams are cost-free aspirations. Goals are dreams with a budget and a plan. Accomplishment of goals is the result of a process of critical thinking about the cost and sequence of action-steps to accomplish a goal, followed by commitment to action. The difference between those who get what they hope for and those who don't is a willingness to make time to work hard on their goals and not just talk about them.

So, when a couple decides to make time to work on their relationship, how can they get the best results? The following is a step-wise process that has worked well for us and others.

Goal-setting for a couple follows exploration of their thoughts, feelings, and desires. You will see how getting to this point requires effective use of asking and listening. As you negotiate and choose shared goals for your marriage, rely on listening and asking to draw each other out and to refine the wording of at least one shared goal that you are both excited and motivated to accomplish.

Don't make this hard. Simply revisit your desires, choose a few that you would like to become reality, and take them through the goal-setting process. As you do, expect to experience hope and joy. Simply thinking about how things might improve in your marriage produces hopeful feelings which grow as you and your spouse take action to actually co-create what was once only an imagined future.

If you are at a loss about some goals you could set, think about where you are in terms of your ability to be emotionally open with each other and the degree of pleasure you have in physical intimacy. In our experience, these are often the two aspects of relationship that couples either celebrate or complain about.[63]

First, have a conversation about desires that you would like to become reality.
- *Ask each other what you want ("I Want," The Desires Exercise). Expand your answers by asking, "What does our marriage want? What would it ask for if it could talk?"*
- *Ask each other about feelings and thoughts associated with the desires.*
- *Reflect what you hear each other say.*
- *Rate the current status of your desires on a scale of 1-10. How much is each currently being fulfilled—with one being a desire that is not fulfilled and ten being a desire that is completely fulfilled?*
- *Pick one desire that is on both of your lists to work on as a shared goal, and pick one on your list that you would like your partner to work on with you (this may take some discussion and negotiation).*

Two Kinds of Goals

Realize as you express your desires and imagine the ideal future that two types of goals are possible:

1. Goals that one of you wants that your partner helps you to achieve.
2. Goals that you both want and that both of you will work to achieve.

No goal is too mundane or trivial. If something is important to one partner then it is important to the other because it is important for the marriage. Remember the US principle. For instance, Jill wanted to plan a great weekend of activities for our oldest daughter's high school graduation. I happened to share Jill's desire, but even if I didn't I would still have listened carefully and put my energy into the action-steps to make the weekend of positive activities a reality because it was important to her. This is a great way to build pleasure—the feeling of love—into your relationship; by fulfilling each other's desires. Helping your partner to accomplish their goals also strengthens the marriage.

After Carly's graduation party I heard some appreciation from Jill. *"Thanks for helping to make this weekend great! I appreciate your hard work."* The point is that positive equity was built into our marriage by our shared efforts to accomplish the very specific goal that we set together. This strengthened our marriage because we each made deposits into each other's love bank. I appreciated Jill's efforts to make my desires a reality, and she appreciated mine. Such ongoing pursuit of goals as a team in marriage will protect you from relationship bankruptcy.

What about a goal that you don't care about? Jill loves yard-work, landscaping and do-it-yourself home projects. But, they're not my first choice for recreation. I'd rather play golf. But because I have decided to care about things that Jill cares about I take care of the yard. Some of you might be saying, "That sounds terrible." Well, it's reality, isn't it? Aren't there things you really care about that your spouse doesn't? Remember, when you are dedicated to cultivating the relationship it will be important to give toward goals that your partner wants and vice versa.

Jill and I realize that some of the difference in what we care about is a function of our different backgrounds before marriage. My father was a college professor who enjoyed sports as recreation. Jill's dad was a farmer and general contractor who relaxed by building and doing maintenance on the family farm. Jill loves to have everything in order and good repair around the house. I want to shoot lower scores on the golf-course, and to ride real far and real fast on a bicycle. How do we handle this? We compromise. I put my heart into her goals and she puts her heart into mine. We've learned to care about what the other cares about. That's love, and it is a great way to strengthen and protect our relationship. But understand there is give and take between us. *We both sacrifice and we both compromise.*

Ultimately it is a rhythm of give and take that protects the bonds of our union by keeping it fresh and fulfilled. I love the smile I see on Jill's face after a home project is completed, and she loves that I come home refreshed and happy after chasing a little white ball around the countryside.

A Word about Godly Goals

Some people struggle with the idea that godly goals can be formed from our desires. Generally, they're suspicious about the changing nature of feelings and humanistic temptations to serve ourselves instead of God. While we applaud such cautiousness, we think that some of our desires are God-given messages to steer our relationships and life goals in the direction that God would have us to go.[64]

How do you know if the goal you are setting is something God wants too? A simple litmus test for godly marriage goals has several components:

1. Does the desire align with something God would want for a married couple?
2. Will it strengthen our marriage?

3. Is it consistent with God's Word?
4. Will fulfillment of the desire somehow be helpful to God's purpose of forming the image of Christ in us?
5. Could accomplishment of the goal somehow be helpful to others?

I (Jeff) once had a Christian counseling client who asked for help with her depression that was complicated by a medical condition. As we approached the end of her therapy, she asked if I would help her with another problem. She wanted to be more sexually compatible (mutually satisfied) with her boyfriend. *"We want to make sure that we'll have a good sex life before we get married."* I told her that morally I couldn't help her with what she was asking because I believe that sex outside of marriage is immoral. Her request didn't line up with the Word of God. Now, if the couple was married and made the same request then I would have been willing to help them to set a goal and to work on it with them.[65] And if they were successful, they would have an authentic testimony they could use to help other couples.

Second, work together to describe your ideal future in relation to that goal (describe specifically what will be happening once the goal is accomplished).

- *Create a picture of what will be happening when your desire(s) are fulfilled? (What will start happening and/or, what will be happening more?)*

Can you imagine it? Is it hard to imagine? Are you there or close to it? If so, what do you think you need to do to keep it? On the other hand, if you're nowhere close, where would be a good place to start?

If you are in a great place we urge you to dream about setting goals to grow your good marriage into a great marriage. And if you aren't very happy or satisfied, we still want to encourage you to dream. Remember, what one couple can do, another can do. Wherever you are, other couples have been there, and have success stories to prove that positive change is possible; even when it was a big mountain to climb.

Here are a few questions to get you thinking:

- *"What does the ideal future look like and feel like in your relationship?"*
- *"What will be happening or won't be happening (or happening more or less) when you are communicating better, feeling more loved, sharing more fun things together?"*
- *"Dream about the ideal future as a couple. What would you like to see, feel and experience in the areas of communication, feeling love, and having fun?"*

Third, articulate it as a S.M.A.R.T. Goal (Specific, Measurable, Achievable, Realistic, and Time-specific).

- *Evaluate that picture for specificity. By when will it be happening? How will you know (measures)? Is it realistic and achievable?*
- *Write and/or speak your goal in three-five sentences. If it is your shared goal, takes turns speaking it until you both agree and feel excited about it. Both of you need to feel good about the way the goal is stated.*

A Few Examples of S.M.A.R.T. Goals

1. *In six weeks we will be able to rate our conflict resolution as an eight on a scale of 1-10 (in comparison to a three now).*
2. *By Christmas we will have completed an addition to our house to the extent that it will be habitable during the cold winter months, meaning that heating and electricity works in the addition even if all decorating is not completed.*
3. *At the end of 60 days we will have completed purchases and organization of his and hers office space so that both are able to work full-time at home with all of the office equipment needed to do our jobs effectively.*

Reading this book is a great first step in educating yourself about how to strengthen and protect your marriage. The next step is the hard work required to realize your goals. *Those of you who assign yourselves to do action-steps to accomplish your goals will be successful!* Don't stop short. Some couples invest significant time and effort in the mutual process of exploration and sharing of their thoughts, feelings and desires but then don't take the next essential step of negotiating and writing out clear, measurable and time-specific goal(s) (i.e., S.M.A.R.T. goals). That's like starting a race and not finishing it. Remember the quote to open chapter one from the fable, "The Tortoise and the Hare," *Perseverance Wins the Race!* Effectively coaching your own marriage requires action!

It's not that identification and expression of honest thoughts, feelings, and desires isn't an end in itself; it is. Honest sharing is an important part of the bonding process. We grow close in relationships as we open our hearts to each other. But, more is possible, and more is needed. We belabor this point because you won't realize your desires for marriage if you stop short of action.[66]

We maintain that any couple that is motivated to grow and change, and willing to take responsibility for the process can make significant strides in healing, strengthening and protecting their marriage. It's worked for us and scores of other couples as we've made time to make things right. And don't forget that key! It takes time to learn any new skill or process. The more you do it, the more natural it will feel, and the more efficient you will be in giving your marriage what it wants and what it needs.

Fourth, brainstorm, evaluate and commit to action-steps to accomplish the goal. It really is this easy, and practice will make it more familiar and efficient.

1. Take one question at a time (i.e. could, want, will).
    a. What *could* you do to begin movement toward actualization of the goal?
        1) Try to generate at least five options. Resist the temptation to evaluate the options at this point. That comes in the next step.

    b. What would you like to do?

       1) Which of the options do you like? What do you like about them?

       2) Which ones do you not like as well, and why?

       3) Rank your options in order of preference. Compare your rank-ordered lists.

    c. What will you do?

       1) Now it's time to decide. Which options do you want to commit to?

       2) Remember, an action-step isn't a legitimate action-step until you commit to a date and time that you are going to do it. Write your action-step(s) in your calendar(s).

Fifth, Write your S.M.A.R.T. Goal on a covenant goal document. (See Appendix D for a sample covenant.)

- *Be sure to chat about the question, "What will accomplishment of this goal mean to our marriage?" Answers to this question stoke motivation and desire to do the action-steps that will fulfill the goal. And it will give you insight into your partner's heart.*

Learning from Jim and Margaret

Jim and Margaret presented a common request from couples: To establish a better process for communication about conflicted topics. Jim admitted being loud during such conversations and that he had trouble sticking to one topic. Margaret reported that she retreated when conversations became loud and angry.

Based on what you learned earlier in this chapter, take notes on the process we facilitated to help them develop a shared goal. Our conversation began by asking them to rate their communication about conflict. Both said about five on a scale of 1-10. *"We can talk about things to a degree, but not to completion."* Coaching questions elicited their thoughts and feelings about how things were in the present. *"We mostly feel frustrated and sad, but sometimes hopeful, because the way we do it now is somewhat better than in the past. We used to rate a zero or one."* Both expressed a desire to be able to rate their communication as a 10.

"What does a 10 look like?" we asked. *"What will observers hear and see when you are doing this at a 10?"* At this point, we facilitated actively listening to each other about their ideal picture, until both expressed that they each felt heard. The next step was a challenge to them to combine their desires into a goal statement. We gave both the opportunity to answer this question, *"If it were up to you to write the goal, including your partner's desires, how would you say it?"* Eventually, after several refinements, they agreed to the following: *"Within six weeks we will conduct conversations about conflicted issues in a way that reaches a mutually satisfying conclusion by Margaret staying in the conversation, even if it gets a little bit heated, and Jim helping by focusing on only one issue at a time, instead of several at the same time."*

Notice that we didn't tell you which one said the goal statement. Why? Because they both said it! They both participated in development of the goal and they both signed off on the final version written above!

Now, let's evaluate the goal. What do you think? Is it S.M.A.R.T.?

It is partially S.M.A.R.T. It is time-specific (six weeks), and it hints at measurability (a mutually satisfying conclusion). The statement would be S.M.A.R.T.er if the measurability was more specific (e.g., 'mutually satisfying conclusion' as evidenced by both Jim and Margaret rating their satisfaction with the conclusion as an eight on a scale of 1-10 for 80% of their conversations).

In other words, a S.M.A.R.T. goal includes a **specific goal** (what will be happening), **a date** by which the change will be happening regularly, and at least a subjective **measure** (e.g., rating on scale, 1-10) or objective measure (evidence that both can see). You might protest, *"That's too complicated!"* Well, maybe it requires careful thinking and a bit more effort than business as usual, but we contend that achievement of meaningful goals is worth it! Our experience is that when you set specific goals you get terrific results!

After they agreed on a clear goal statement, the next step for Jim and Margaret was to make a list of as many possible things they could do to work toward accomplishing their goal. Then they discussed and evaluated their action-steps by actively listening to each other. During this step they both were free to share which options they liked and which ones they didn't, and why.[67] This is a critical part of action-step development for buy-in to the action plan, and it keeps the process realistic.

Potential action-steps aren't created equal. Some won't be feasible and others won't be desirable. Therefore, it is imperative for a couple to have a thorough evaluative discussion during which they elicit and hear one another's thoughts and feelings about the steps they could take. The ultimate razor to make decisions about which action-steps to do is according to what a couple's marriage wants and what it needs. When that question is considered, the individual partners have an easier time choosing and doing action-steps because they remember that they are serving an entity greater than self; their marriage.

The final step for Jim and Margaret was to negotiate which steps that *both* were willing to do and a plan to do them. They wrote the steps they chose into their calendar, taking care to estimate the amount of time it would take to do them. This fulfilled the criteria which states that, *"An action-step isn't legitimate until you can write it on your calendar."*

A Few of Their Action-Steps

- "Every morning before leaving for work, we will ask each other (take turns) if there are any conflicts or emotional topics that would be good for us to make time to talk about (note: we won't necessarily talk about it then, but we will at least acknowledge if there is something that we need to talk about).
- The person with the topic will estimate how much time will be needed to discuss the topic to completion. That same person will propose a time to have the conversation.

- The person being asked for the conversation will agree to the proposed time or duration, or will explain why that time doesn't work and will propose an alternative time.

(Note: Jim and Margaret had several other action-steps, including an agreement to write a summary reflection of how they experienced the conversation including what was positive about the conversation and any suggestions for such conversations to go better in the future.)

An Effective Process

Setting effective goals is the nitty-gritty of the process of coaching your marriage. It might seem tedious to get so specific about the components of a S.M.A.R.T. goal, and it might seem laborious to negotiate action-steps, but *this is where the process of coaching your own marriage proves its effectiveness; in the specificity of goals and action-steps, and clear commitment to do everything it takes to heal, strengthen and protect your marriage.* We didn't say this would be easy, but we did promise that it would be worthwhile.

Make no mistake that the coaching approach to marriage requires significant effort. This is because it is highly action-oriented. You actually act on the things you talk about. That requires time and effort. If there is bad news, that's it. It requires real effort. Remember, in coaching we say that if goals are not being set, and action-steps aren't being done, it isn't coaching; it is merely conversation. The litmus test for an effective coaching process is accomplishment of goals.

But, the Great News is that it is effective. *It will work if you work it!*

CHAPTER EIGHT
Reflection Questions:

1. What do you think about our assertion that setting goals is a responsive act of worship; that it is good stewardship of the desires that God has put in your heart to fulfill His vision for your marriage?

_____

_____

_____

_____

_____

2. Do you find it easy or difficult to identify and express your desires? If it is difficult, what could your spouse do (or refrain from doing) that would help you to more freely tell them what you want?

_____

_____

_____

_____

_____

3. How do you hope it will it impact your marriage to pursue some goals together?

_____

_____

_____

_____

_____

Support, Encouragement & Accountability

Any degree of change in human behavior is difficult. Systems don't change easily and neither do our habits. Once patterns are set and habits are established, a lot of energy is required to form new ones. Think about the time it takes for a ship to change direction or for a big truck or train to slow to a stop and turn around. The laws of physics say that objects in motion tend to stay in motion and that objects at rest tend to stay at rest. The same is true in relationships. It is easier to keep doing what you have been doing than it is to do new things. New ways of being and relating require the application of vast amounts of time and energy. But it's worth it.

To help you understand the process of change in human behavior, think about one of the most challenging goals that you have accomplished in your life. Maybe it's successfully completing a marathon, obtaining an academic degree or weathering an unusually difficult season of life? How about having a successful marriage? That one is at the top of the list of most challenging goals for a lot of people. Pause now to identify that challenging goal you accomplished—either in your relationship with your spouse or any other area in your life. Keeping that goal in mind will help you understand the nature and importance of relational support, encouragement and accountability (SEA) in successfully accomplishing goals—essential ingredients to keep us energized and motivated to do the action-steps we've chosen to achieve our goal.

To understand how SEA works, think about the challenging goal you accomplished. Did you accomplish it completely on your own, or were there other people who came alongside you as supporters and encouragers? Whose support and encouragement was essential for you to accomplish your goal? Perhaps it was a parent, a teacher, a coach or a friend? Perhaps it was your spouse? Hopefully, there were several people involved in the process. Looking back, what did their practical gestures of support and words of encouragement mean to you?

We'll illustrate this with a story from our marriage. Jill and I practically grew up together. We met as teenagers, and tied the knot at 20 and 21 years old (I'm not saying who is older). We married during my junior year of college just after Jill finished her degree, so she moved to my college town where we set up our first home. During the day, she worked for a group of optometrists, and I went to school. In the evenings I studied, and she often helped me by typing lengthy research papers and projects. Word processors were rare at the time, but we had a great typewriter. The challenge was making the papers perfect for presentation to a demanding research psychology professor. One mistake and the typist had to start over since correction tape or "white out" was prohibited. Many nights we were up late. I wrote by hand, and Jill typed. This practical gesture of support had everything to do with the completion of my undergrad degree in psychology. I couldn't have done it without her. In addition, Jill encouraged me to persevere: *This is a step in the direction of doing what you were born to do. I believe in you and want to see you fulfill your potential.* I can't imagine accomplishing my undergrad degree without her practical support and encouraging gestures. A testimony to her character and steadfastness is that she continued to support and encourage me through a graduate degree too.

What does this story make you think about from your life? Which accomplishment comes to mind that at least one other person had a part of through the support and encouragement they provided?

Support

The first letter in the SEA equation is S for Support. We define support as practical gestures that others do to help us reach our goals. It is primarily their behavior, not their words that communicate their desire to see us succeed. It's a message communicated through behavior: "I want you to accomplish this goal, and so I am going to do things to help you." One gentleman I know remembers his wife baking cookies, brewing coffee and rubbing his shoulders during his long evenings of study for his Ph.D. He told me that she didn't have to say anything. Her actions communicated to him that she believed in him and wanted him to earn the degree. *"Many nights I was tempted to shut the books and quit the program, but her love and support expressed in practical ways kept me going."*

Last winter I supported Jill in her goal to improve her fitness and to reduce back pain by doing a daily video routine with her. Nearly every day for three months, we descended the stairs to the basement where we knew that heavy breathing and burning muscles were minutes away. There were days I would have rather gone to the gym by myself, gone for a bike ride or not exercised at all, but I heard her loud and clear about how much she enjoyed doing the program with me, and how helpful it was to her being consistent on the plan for me to push her to do it. My desire to help her to achieve her goal was the primary motivator that fueled my supportive behaviors.

Practically speaking, I would initiate the scheduling of a time to do the workout, move the furniture in the family room, get towels and water bottles and start the DVD.[68] Later she said that all of the things I did to consistently push to continue the daily workouts and to model stamina during the workouts were essential to her continuing the program. There were several great results: 1. We got in great shape, 2. We grew in respect for each other as athletes, 3. We learned to suffer together and how to encourage and motivate each other during physical discomfort (that came into play during some third world travel the following summer), 4. We grew as givers by giving support and encouragement to each other during a very strenuous endeavor, and 5. Her back pain was resolved!

Tips on Providing Support

- **Give with a good attitude** – Give with a positive and willing attitude or don't give at all. "God loves a cheerful giver" and so does your spouse. They can tell if you are giving from the heart, or giving out of a sense of obligation. More than half of the benefit I experience as a recipient of Jill's support when I'm working on a goal is the attitude with which she gives. When she gives cheerfully I catch her enthusiasm for what I'm working on in addition to the practical help she provides by her gesture of support.

- **Give without expectation of getting something in return** – "It is more blessed to give than receive." Give from an unselfish heart. Giving to get isn't giving. It's bartering. Give with no expectation of receiving something in return. Free the recipient of your support to focus on attainment of the goal instead of burdening them with a bill they have to pay for your support.

- **Give when you are prompted to give** – Listen to the intuition and discernment that comes to you in a quiet voice with an idea of something you can do to demonstrate support to your partner. This is often a way God prompts timely and needed gestures of support. Try to act on the prompt as soon as possible so that you don't talk yourself out of the idea.

- **Give till it hurts** – When you love someone, giving has no end. As long as they are on the path to complete a goal that you support, or a shared goal that you are working on together, support is important. Can you give too much? Can you give too often?

- **Give even when they're grouchy** – Love isn't conditional so support shouldn't be either. After all, support is a practical form of love; giving is relevant to the goal your partner is pursuing.

- **Give what you would like to be given** – When you aren't sure how to support your partner, ask yourself what you would like to receive if you were in their shoes. *What would be meaningful to me? What would I appreciate?*

- **Give what they would like to receive** – If all else fails, simply ask your partner how you could support them or help them. I love being asked this question. It's like being handed a blank check with an opportunity to write in the amount I need. My partner is offering to give what I need to keep going? Jill often asks such questions when she sees that I have a busy day of appointments, *"What can I do for you?"* My answer, *"Fix some lunch, make some calls, give me a hug…"* Just her willingness to support me helps gives me strength and willingness to keep working.

In your life, consider how others, including your spouse, have supported you in the pursuit of some of your goals. What did their support mean to you?

Encouragement

The second letter in the SEA equation is E for Encouragement. Whereas support is helpful behavior, encouragement is expressed in words. As I've been writing this book the following words from three people ring in my ears: *"You know you have to get this book done to help more couples like us."*[69] *"God has gone to great lengths to give you experience and information that can be helpful to a lot of people. Getting it into a book is good stewardship of what God has given to you."*[70] *"We know how much our instruction has helped the couples we've shared it with. Just get it written down, and I'll read it, reflect on it, make editing suggestions and write the portions you want me to write."*[71] As their encouragements echoed in my mind, I experienced a deeper degree of determination to get it done!

In Our Marriage

Verbal encouragement played a role in helping both Jill and I to persist in the P90X® fitness program, day after day, week after week. Both of us sincerely complimented each other on good technique, urged each other to make it to the end of the workout and offered sincere compliments for the progress we noticed that each of us was making, *"Good job! Way to go finishing that set of exercises today. That's more than last time, and you're doing it with intensity!"* It's amazing how much it helps to keep you going when someone tells you that you are doing something well and that they believe you can make it to the end.

From Other Marriages for Your Marriage

Jill and I have participated on a weekly prayer call with four other couples since 2006. Often before we do seminars we ask for prayer for our marriage and the couples we will be serving. Our friends never fail to encourage us as we prepare. They say things like, *"You have everything in your minds and hearts that God wants you to have for this opportunity to minister. Be yourselves and trust Him. We've seen you do this, and you'll be great!"* Support like that never gets old, and it always helps us to feel confident and at peace as we experience new people in new situations.

The unique power of relational encouragement comes from the fact that it is provided by people who deeply care about us living out the fullness of who God has made us to be and to do the things He created us to do. Relational encouragement conveys the basic message that failure is not an option when it comes to fulfilling your God-given purpose and potential. Those who encourage us effectively communicate, *"I see who you are, and I affirm what you have been made to do. Like it or not, I'm going to be a loving thorn in your side to remind you, encourage you, and even lovingly confront you if you get off track, distracted, or lose heart."* Why? Because your contribution to the Kingdom of God is unique, and it is essential!

Tips for Encouraging Words

- **Pray for encouraging words** – Lord, what would you have me say? What would encourage her/him? Go to the one who knows your spouse better than you for words to encourage them.

- **Say what you mean and mean what you say** – Don't say something just to be saying something. If it's not from your heart your partner will probably be able to tell. Reflect on what you want to say before you say it. Ask yourself, *"Do I really, really mean this?"*

- **Be prepared to back your words with action** – Faith without works is dead, and actions speak louder than words. Are you willing to support your words with sacrifice? During a recent trip to India a young couple attended one of our "How to Coach Your Marriage Seminars". Later we learned how they were invited and the lengths to which the person who invited them went to make it possible for them to attend. *"Marianne called to say that we would be a great couple to take the training that follows the seminar and that she really believed in our marriage. We wanted to come but didn't have a babysitter, so she volunteered, on the spur of the moment to watch our five kids for the entire evening!"*

- **Be prepared to minister** – How does your spouse respond to encouraging words? Do they receive from you in humility, or do they argue with you, *"No, I'm not"* or *"No, I can't"*. Be prepared to engage a level of spiritual warfare in prayer and perhaps conversation or prophetic ministry to release them from bondage of lies that the enemy has told them and that they have believed. We're not saying that there is a demon behind every discouragement or disbelief about one's ability to accomplish a goal, but it does seem clear that it would be the enemy and not God who would want us to falter and fail.

- **Consider what you might like to hear** – Often people are at a loss about what to say to encourage others. A great way to come up with ideas is to ask yourself what you might like to hear if you were pursuing that goal. After you come up with some answers, pray over them to see if you feel a prompt with peace to say it.

Is your partner working on a goal, or are you working together on a goal? What do you respect, appreciate or admire about the way they are working toward that goal? Don't assume they know what you think. Pray over your answers and then give them the gift of encouraging words.

Accountability

The A in the SEA formula stands for accountability. It combines support, encouragement and even loving confrontation if we depart from a path we once said that we wanted to walk. Accountability always works best when we ask for it.

Unfortunately, accountability has a taken a bad rap in some circles. That's because it is sometimes practiced in an unhealthy way; as an excuse to take control of someone's life. Here's an illustration of a healthy version of accountability.

Suppose I set a goal to write fourteen hours per week, and I make myself accountable to Jill and our weekly couple's prayer group. A healthy way to do this, as a person who takes responsibility for my life, is to volunteer to report on how well I've met my goal for the week instead of waiting to be asked. This keeps me in charge of my life while providing the benefit of watchful and caring eyes to observe my progress on a goal I'm motivated to accomplish. This version of accountability helps me to feel like an adult responsible for my own life instead of a child that begrudgingly does what he is supposed to do out of fear of reprisal.

Tony Stolzfus has written extensively about healthy accountability as an opportunity to stand in for Jesus who invites us to grow and change rather than attempting to mandate change by trying to control our life.[72] Consider how Jesus invited the rich young ruler to follow him and how he invites all who are weary to come to him. He didn't collar the ruler to make him follow, and he doesn't commandeer control of our lives against our will. Thus, when we stand in for Jesus in other's lives, we follow his example by inviting them to the opportunity to volunteer for accountability to do the things they say they want to do!

Let me make this clearer with a further illustration. I coached a husband who had a goal to be his best self in conversations with his wife. The challenge was that his wife was intense and verbally eloquent. It was hard for him to get in a word edge-wise, and his responses were sometimes quickly rejected and scorned. But still, his goal was to stand up to her in the strength of his masculinity, appropriately. He didn't want to fight fire with fire, but neither did he want to retreat in self-protective hopelessness. So, he chose the goal of staying in emotional conversations with his wife, both mentally and physically.

Our conversation about accountability went like this: *"I want to stay in the room and continue to try to reflect what she says and to interject my perspective and desires,"* he said.

"When will be your next opportunity to do this?" I asked.

"Tonight, we agreed to try to talk after supper."

"Would accountability be helpful?" I asked.

"Yes," he quickly responded.

"Well, would you be willing to take responsibility to let me know how it goes after you accomplish your goal this evening?" I asked.

"Yes, that feels good. Instead of you checking on me, I will take responsibility to send an email tomorrow morning to tell you how it went."

Notice that he had a choice about accountability, and that he is the one taking initiative to report on the success of his goal.

When we offer accountability to others we serve them in two ways:
1. Ongoing encouraging reminders about what they said they wanted to do.
2. Understanding and compassionate confrontation when they miss a deadline for a commitment to do something they said they wanted to do.

Ongoing reminders are a mix of encouragement and accountability. I'll often send a text or voicemail to say, *"I've been thinking and praying for you in this endeavor. Just wanted you to know I believe in you, and I'm looking forward to hearing your joy as you see progress toward your goal."* When others do that for me it's a reminder that loving, caring and invested eyes are watching, *Oh yeah* I say to myself. *I'd better get on that.* Jill will admit that I was the one to drive the P90X® program more than her. When we began she was regular, and she even reminded me that it was time to do the workout, *"Come on buddy. This is good for us."* But as weeks passed, she groaned a bit, *"Do we have to?"* It was then that I reminded her that it was helping her back and that she was always glad she'd done the workout when it was over. *"You said you've got to do something like this for your upper body strength, honey. Come on. Plus, it's good for me and encourages me to do it together."*

Compassionate confrontation comes into play when a person misses a deadline to report progress or completion of a commitment. The first thing I do in that situation is to remember how many times I've missed a deadline and why. Sometimes life interfered, and sometimes I got distracted or lost motivation. Then I remember how my favorite coaches engaged me with accountability. In a word it's grace.

The compassionate accountability partner believes the best about you; that you want to accomplish the goals you've set, and that you are capable of achieving them. They mix compassionate understanding with tenacious determination to see you through the finish line. Their courage to challenge you comes from loving desire to see you become a more capable leader of your own life and to fulfill your God-given destiny.

There were several times during the winter workout regime that Jill and my schedule simply didn't permit us to do the workout together. I usually found a way to work it in, but she took a pass a couple of times. When I heard her hedge about getting back in the routine the next day I told her that I understood that life was interfering and it may be hard, but still wanted to encourage her to find a way to do at least part of the workout by herself. She appreciated this; especially because before we ever began the program she told me that she wanted me to keep her accountable to finish it. She'd given me her blessing and permission to keep her accountable.

In the purest sense, the person that provides accountability stands in for Jesus who calls you forward as one who also struggled to accomplish His purpose. Though it was a struggle He did, and so can you do by his life within you! The ideal accountability partner knows all this and brings it to bear on you in a way that resonates with your life purpose, helps you to regroup and revive, and to move forward in confidence instead of wallowing in failure and despair. Please keep this manner and spirit of accountability in mind as you consider these tips:

Ask, *"Would accountability be helpful?"* – This question brings the issue of accountability to awareness and indicates that a person has freedom to choose whether or not to be accountable. It is a respectful question that honors the right of a person to choose how to work on a goal, even if it is your spouse ... especially if it is your spouse. While you might have a vested interest in them achieving the goal they're working on (e.g., listening more attentively, responding with a more patient and kind tone of voice, cleaning out the garage, etc.) that doesn't mean you have the right to try to control their behavior. And just because they say that it would be helpful to have accountability doesn't mean that you will get to be the one to provide it. You simply asked if it would be helpful as your way of being faithful to the final step of goal achievement; the establishment of SEA.

If they answer yes, ask, *"Who would you like to be accountable to?"* – Often the answer will be "you". It makes sense because you probably know a lot about the goal and the reason(s) they want to achieve it. But they may say another friend, co-worker, etc. Don't take that personally. Just be glad that they are including this essential ingredient for goal attainment in their formula for success.

Ask, *"How would you like to report your progress?"* – This question begins to move toward a specific action-step. If it's their spouse, they can simply tell you in person. If it is someone else, they may suggest writing an email, writing a text or leaving a message on voicemail. When I'm chosen for accountability I write the date on the calendar that the person has promised to report on their progress.

Ask, *"What would you like me (or another accountability partner) to do if I don't hear from you?"* – It is always good to establish this back-up plan in advance, and to have a person's blessing to come looking for them if they become silent about their goal and the action-steps they committed to do. That way, when you call, write or knock on their door it's within the boundaries of the agreement you made before and won't be perceived as you trying to make them change or to accomplish something that you want and they don't.

Assume the best when you ask accountability questions – The first thing I do when presented the opportunity to serve a client or friend with accountability is to remember the times I've failed to meet deadlines or to accomplish action-steps or a goal. This helps me to be compassionate to the myriad of reasons that a person may be lagging. I also remember that God is ultimately in charge to inspire and move others to action, and that He may have made a mid-course correction or introduced something into a person's life that He wants them to invest energy in rather than the goal they'd set. In other words, approach the conversation believing the best about a person; that they meant what they said about their goal, but that for some reason something has changed. Then be prepared to serve them in processing that change, to regroup, re-focus and to move forward.

A Shared Goal

In 2004 Jill and I transitioned from working together in a full-time Christian counseling practice to work as a team of two to develop a community marriage initiative. Part of the challenge of developing a non-profit ministry together was learning to work together in a new way. We quickly discovered that we needed to develop a set of communication and conflict resolution skills to work effectively as a team.

After a few frustrating episodes of miscommunication we set a goal to work through conflict in a way that felt respectful and loving to both of us. We demonstrated our support to each other by sharing the initiative to schedule times to talk and by taking turns going to each other's offices for those conversations. When I sat in Jill's office I offered to abide by her preference for a slower paced and more detail oriented conversation. When she came to my office she offered bullet points of information in quick succession. We both took notes on tasks that the other needed us to do. In other words an observer would have easily been able to recognize supportive behaviors that communicated desire to accomplish the goal of communicating clearly and working through conflict. We also said encouraging words to each other: *"I like how we had that conversation,"* or *"I think we are learning how to patiently communicate about our different perspectives in a respectful way."*

As we successfully pursued our goal, the reality was that each of us was the best supporter and best encourager for the other. It wasn't an easy goal to achieve, though. There were times that we both became frustrated to the point of quitting, *"This is too hard! Not only is the work really hard, but it's also hard to work with you!"* We're thankful that we persevered; not only because of what was accomplished externally in the ministry, but also because we grew stronger and healthier as a team of two as we learned to love each other by honoring our respective differences and meeting each other's needs.

The fact that you are reading this book is proof that we have continued to persevere through situational challenges and frustrations. We mention this to encourage you as you face challenges in your marriage, especially if you are learning to work together to help other couples.[73]

Envisioning the end goals of working together and seeing results from our efforts to help marriages inspired and motivated us to continue working on our goals. Celebrations of intermediate success were encouraging. Reframing conflicts as opportunities to learn about ourselves and each other helped us to have more positive feelings about inevitable conflicts. Support, encouragement and accountability from each other and others was like a push up a hill when we felt exhausted. It kept us going when we wanted to quit, and eventually we crossed the finish line.

As we continue to embrace opportunities to grow and change, we realize that we are becoming a stronger couple and that each victory adds to our collection of authentic illustrations to inspire and equip others.

A Sustainable Pace

The journey of marriage isn't a sprint, but rather a paced marathon. It's a long journey in which we must persevere on a daily basis. Do you recall the memorable line from Aesop's fable, The Tortoise and The Hare: "Steady wins the race"?

There is a lot of power in what others think you are capable of doing. When Jill or a friend tells me that I'm good at something or that they believe in me, it often gives me the boost in energy and motivation I need to keep trying.

What keeps me going during long periods of writing? One thing is a reminder that I provide to myself that it will probably help to make a difference in other's lives. But important additional sources of encouragement come from others. For instance, Jill encourages me with words by telling me that she admires my work ethic and determination to get things done. She urges me to press on, *"This is going to help explain what we've learned about how to help relationships."* In addition, she shows her support for our writing goals by giving me long periods of privacy. She refrains from interrupting these periods and protects me from interruption by others (e.g., phone calls). Finally, she keeps me accountable to what I've said I'm going to get done, which is something I ask for by telling her how much I want to complete and by when. Periodically she checks on my progress, which is helpful if I begin to feel like quitting because I say to myself, *I want to keep my word to her.*

On your marriage journey you can find daily opportunities to support and encourage your partner. After all, the race you're in is a race you are doing together, like a three-legged race. As you support and encourage your partner, they in turn will support and encourage you. Together you run a sustainable pace in unison toward the finish line, keeping your vows and perpetually engaging the never-ending process of growth and change, till death do you part.

CHAPTER NINE
Reflection Questions:

1. How did it impact you to think about the role of relational Support, Encouragement and Accountability in your major accomplishments?

_____

_____

_____

_____

_____

2. Which is easiest for you to give to your spouse; Support in loving and supportive gestures, Encouragement in words, or Accountability as gentle and loving challenge to persist in goals they've set?

_____

_____

_____

_____

_____

3. Which is most helpful for you to receive when you are pursuing a goal or working on your part of a shared goal; S, E or A?

_____

_____

_____

_____

_____

Jeff & Jill's Marriage Tips

Even if learning to coach your marriage goes as well as possible it probably won't be easy and won't go smoothly, but it will be worthwhile. The *bad news* is that it takes time to integrate this process into your relationship. The *good news* is that many couples have gone before you, and have found the results to be worth the effort.[74] So now that you have done your due diligence of reading, reflecting and practicing loving listening, curious asking, effective goal-setting, and learning how to include the elements of SEA you may have some questions about the process, or you may have run into some obstacles or challenges as you try to implement it. This doesn't surprise us. While this is a simple process it isn't easy. Emotions get involved and the circumstances of life are complex.

In this chapter we will address some of the most frequently asked questions couples ask us as they learn Marriage Coaching and begin to coach their own marriage. If we had an hour to sit down with you personally, the following tips are the ones we would reiterate to give you the best chance to heal, strengthen and protect your marriage.

Tip One: It will work if you work it.

While coaching your marriage might appear to be an easy process, we urge you to not mistake simple with easy. At first glance you might think, *Listening, asking, setting goals? That's so simple.* Yes, but emotions, history and assumptions complicate the process. Our internal dialogue is much faster than the spoken word, so most of us who have been in relationship for any length of time make assumptions about what our partner is going to say, what they feel and how they think about things. Jumping to conclusions may seem like a shortcut, but our experience is that it slows down and complicates the process of reaching shared understanding. It's better to go slowly in order to listen and reflect carefully, than to jump ahead. More times than not, jumping ahead results in a need to backtrack to clear up misunderstandings.

Many couples that invest time to learn the principles and practices of Marriage Coaching determine that it could help them. But it won't work if you don't make time to work on it. It's like buying state of the art exercise equipment and then not making time to use it. The sad confession from couples that don't make progress very quickly goes like this, *"We haven't made time to use the process." "What are your results so far?"* we ask. *"Not very good,"* they reply. *"Yep, that's about right. It won't work unless you work it."*

Some of you need to get really serious about investing time and energy into working the process, because business as usual isn't likely to cut it when you are trying to establish new patterns and habits of communication. Look at your schedule of commitments in terms of what is necessary for your daily life (sleep, eating, working, etc.) and what is optional. Hobbies, including social and some recreational/athletic activities fall under the optional category. I (Jeff) once lost a bicycling buddy for three years because he jettisoned all optional activities to work on his marriage. His reasoning was that he could eventually return to cycling, but that he had only one chance to save his marriage. He didn't want to look back with regret that he'd not done everything possible to put all of his energies into this top priority. His strategy worked! His wife even now blesses him to train for triathlons so don't think that if you give yourself to a season of intensive effort to integrate this process in marriage that it's all you will ever do.

So the question is, when are you going to make time to do this? When are you going to MAKE time to have quality conversations? Increasingly, this is the first topic we cover when coaching couples or presenting seminars. Remember your dating relationship? Most couples easily recall how they invested hours in conversation getting to know each other. But then life happens; career, kids, community activities ... and many couples don't make as much time to talk.

"We grew apart," they tell us as part of their explanation about why they are separated or considering divorce. *Note: The same formula that you used to grow together in the first place can help you to grow back together.* Make time to have quality conversations using the skills of curious asking and loving listening. You will be pleasantly surprised by how quickly the feeling of love reappears as you make time to hear and hold each other's hearts.

Tip Two: The more emotional the conversation, the more you need good skills.

Emotional topics are like minefields for many couples. One misstep blows things up and makes a mess. Think about this analogy. If you had to walk through a minefield, how would you do it? *Slowly, carefully and skillfully.* Picking your way through territory fraught with potential disaster at a slow pace with great care would give you the best chance of survival. When things get heated SLOW DOWN! Live to fight another day!

The more heated a conversation, the more important it is to turn down the temperature of conflict by slowing things down. Such conversations can sneak up on you, so be prepared. React with patient and unselfish loving listening on a moment's notice. It is the first and best way to respond when you're ambushed by unpleasant emotion within yourself or from your partner. In fact, the survival of your relationship may depend on you doing this. Slow things down. Hear and hold your partner's heart! Accident victims who suffer severe physical trauma have a better chance of survival when they are treated in operating rooms with cooler temperatures.[75] One effect of the cooler temperatures is that hemorrhaging is slowed.

We haven't met a marriage that doesn't experience strong emotions around certain topics (e.g., parenting, finances, sex, extended family, etc.). Some couples habitually avoid these topics and/or withhold their honest thoughts, feelings and desires from any conversation around these topics. But that isn't true intimacy, and it usually results in one partner having things the way they want while the other continues to live with a container full of suppressed resentment and dissatisfaction. When this dynamic surfaces during a coaching session, we usually hear that this is the way the marriage has evolved "to keep the peace". But while the external peace is maintained, internal peace is disturbed because suppression of one's honest thoughts, feelings and desires comes at the price of authentic intimacy, shared understanding and respect for each other's perspective, emotions and desires. It is only through skillful and loving exploration of these issues that real, lasting and pleasurable intimacy is accomplished.

Tip Three: If you can't have a conversation in a good way, don't have the conversation.

How many times have you plunged ahead into a difficult conversation while a voice in the back of your mind says STOP? In the moment it can feel good to let a barrage of angry words fly, or to speak to sensitive issues in a rough way without much forethought, but there is usually a heavy price to be paid in hurt feelings and broken trust. When you feel a check in your spirit about the way you are about to have a conversation (or about continuing if it is beginning to go badly), call for a time-out to regroup. Pray, reflect, journal, work through your emotions, and consider some alternatives for continuing the conversation in a way that will protect and build your relationship instead of hurting it.

"Do over's" were one of the rules my childhood friends and I stipulated at the beginning of a game. We either decided to play with or without them, and also how many would be allowed for each participant. In our marriage we ask for "do over's" when a conversation begins to deteriorate due to misunderstandings or when one of us realizes that what we've said or the way we said it isn't accurate or kind. Many times we ask for a "do over" the next day after an unpleasant exchange. It's like hitting the reset button on a video game to begin again because the game has gotten out of hand or you've made a mistake. It provides a fresh opportunity to try again. Oh, and in the marriage game we recommend an unlimited number of "do-over's".

Tip Four: Decide what's best for US when you don't agree.

Sometimes you will feel stuck between opposing options. You want to talk but he doesn't. He wants to make love but you don't. She wants to socialize by having some friends over, but you would rather have the evening to yourselves. What to do? Either compromise by creating a solution that provides both of you with a bit of what you want or die to your desires so that your partner will be completely fulfilled.

One way Jill and I work through competing desires is to ask what's good for our marriage and what our marriage needs. If our marriage could speak, what would it ask for? These questions help us to take a step back from self to observe the union of our partnership. Would it be good for our relationship to have some time to talk, to take a walk, to make love, to socialize with an encouraging set of friends, to minister together, etc.? This moves our minds beyond what self wants to a more objective analysis about what is healthy and helpful to heal, strengthen and protect our relationship and/or what will help us to experience pleasure (the feeling of love) and to live our purpose.

Another way to think about this is the phrase *lowest common denominator*. Go with the easier, less demanding and more grace oriented option. For instance, you want to resolve a conflict now, but he/she doesn't. They need rest before they are ready to be their best. Respect the needs of the partner that represents the lowest common denominator rather than pushing them to suck it up to do the hard thing even though they're not ready. On the other hand, if they volunteer to submit to your desire, go with that. The lowest common denominator is a guideline, not a hard and fast rule.

Tip Five: The process of communication is more important than the content.

Daily life calls for decisions and solutions to problems. When deadlines are imminent, it can be tempting to compromise good process that takes time. This is nearly always a huge mistake for the relationship. Good process protects and strengthens relationships by investing time to ask and listen to each other to achieve shared understanding about respective desires. Ensure that both of you have an opportunity to share what is in your heart and mind. Realize that as you practice good process you will become more efficient. Work toward the goal of being able to say, *"I like how we talked about that"*. Or *"I like that we both shared and heard each other's perspectives before we made a decision"*.

We frequently see couples experiencing unnecessary pain and conflict because they hurried through a discussion or decision-making process in order to meet someone else's deadline. But just because someone else has a crisis doesn't mean that it needs to become your crisis. It is paramount to honor a life-giving process of communication in your marriage. Thus we encourage you to get comfortable asking others to wait for decisions that impact both you and your spouse instead of hurrying through a partial discussion or not having a discussion and one of you making a unilateral decision (that's even worse!). Children, bosses and ministry colleagues can learn to wait for you and your spouse to work through a good process for your relationship regarding decisions that affect them. Realize that when you refuse to be hurried through discussion and decision-making that you are not only doing something good for your marriage but also for others as you practice and model a healthy process that others might need to integrate into their own relationships.

Tip Six: Talk about talking before you talk.

When you answer the phone do you appreciate being asked if it is a good time to talk? I do. I especially like it when the caller shares the topic, their objective for the conversation, the approximate duration, and whether or not there is a deadline. *"Jeff, I need to talk with you about Carly's financial aid for college. It will probably take 10-15 minutes to share an update about what the school has proposed and the options we have to make up the difference."* This gives me all the information I need to decide whether to have the conversation right then or to ask Jill to wait until a more convenient time.

Such a formal approach to conversations in marriage isn't common. Our observation is that married couples are more likely to charge into each other's presence without regard for what their partner is doing, or consideration of whether or not it is a good time to have a conversation. And this simple lack of respect and courtesy is often the culprit behind conversations that go poorly.

The solution is simple. Make it a habit of courtesy to ask your partner if you can interrupt them for a moment. Then present the topic of conversation, the expected duration, and the ideal deadline if the topic is time-sensitive. Be pleasantly surprised if they agree to the conversation right away, but also be willing to wait if they don't want to talk at that moment. If there is good-will between you, what comes around will go around. You will receive what you give. Give courtesy, get courtesy.

Tip Seven: Be participant-observers.

Remember that your marriage is the object of your efforts as you coach your relationship. Some growth goals can be discovered through your personal desires, and others can be discovered by stepping back to observe what your marriage needs (e.g., "If our marriage could speak, what would it ask for?"). It's obvious that we are participants in marriage, but we can also be observers of the relationship. It is especially helpful during challenging seasons to objectively observe the relationship and what is happening between us. If we observed the same things happening in another relationship, what would we think and what would we recommend?

Tip Eight: Turn off the conversation in your head.

How often do you find yourself lost in a conversation because you took off down a "bunny trail" to chase some thoughts related to something your partner just said? Or, how often do you find yourself wanting to complete your partner's sentences because you assume that you know what they are going to say next? Misunderstandings occur frequently when we have two conversations at the same time; one with our partner and the one with ourselves about what they are saying.

Stopping internal conversations isn't easy, so we invoke supernatural help, *"Jesus, please quiet my mind. Help me to relax in listening, and to practice the disciplines of asking and listening without assumptions of meaning. I want to understand what my wife/husband really means, and not just what I think they mean. In Jesus' name. Amen."*

There are some other practical things we can do as well, such as refraining from texting, reading, or watching television while we are listening to our partner. Anything that opens another window in our mind compromises the depth of our focus on our partner and the fullness of what they are attempting to communicate to us. When we are distracted in a conversation, it communicates to the other person that they are not as important as the other thing that is vying for our attention. Fail to focus on your spouse long enough and often enough and you may not have a spouse for very long.

Tip Nine: Ask, don't tell.

When you feel like giving advice, pause to ask yourself if there is a way you could ask a question instead. Work to open your partner's heart by asking about their thoughts, feelings and desires as often as possible, and withhold your opinion or advice unless or until they ask for it. This may seem impractical as a hard and fast rule. If so, we suggest at least asking if they would like to hear your thoughts or advice before you give it.

Wonder and keep wondering what your partner thinks, how they feel and what they might want. Don't assume that you know. Be willing to ask. When they share concerns and experiences with you, ask questions to get them to share their perspective and emotions. If you have trouble with motivation to do this, ask yourself, *How do I feel when I'm asked what I think or how I feel about something?*

Tip Ten: Take turns.

Recall the principle of math in Marriage Coaching. In math, what you do on one side of the equation needs to be done on the other side. In marriage, both partners must have a turn to be heard and understood. You'll get your turn after your partner is done with their turn. Usually it's after you have listened well with good heart. The more sincere and focused you are, the sooner you'll get a turn. Give well and you will receive well.

Another way to look at it is that you will get your turn when it is good for your relationship for you to take your turn. Sometimes challenging conversations require a significant investment of effort and energy. Both of you might need a break to reflect and to restore energies before more conversation. If you find yourself at that place, take a step back from your relationship to consider whether taking your turn immediately after you partner will be good for your relationship. Note: This is different than asking and deciding that you would LIKE to take your turn. You might want to, but it might not be good. Err on the side of caution to protect your relationship by making rational decisions about when the listening partner will have their turn to talk.

Your partner's condition is an additional factor that can affect the decision when to take your turn. One of you might be struggling with a health issue, an extended family situation that affects one of you more than the other, career discouragement or disillusionment; in a word grief. Marriage isn't always 50/50. There are times/seasons when one partner may need more listening and asking. It isn't always about a fair balance between you but more about what your marriage needs.

Tip Eleven: What to do if you think your partner is wrong.

If your partner is sharing their feelings then they can't be wrong. By definition, feelings aren't wrong or right. Now, they might be based on wrong thinking or misperceptions, but they still aren't wrong.

But what if the way your partner remembers a situation is wrong? When you ask this question it suggests that you think that you have a perfect memory, and that the way you remember a conversation or situation is the right way; that you have perfect recall. What if you do? Can you convince your partner by asserting your perspective more loudly or repeatedly? Probably not, so how can the stalemate be resolved?

Here's a fun exercise to support this point. Hold a cell phone up between two people sitting face to face. Make sure that the dial pad or touch screen is facing one person and the back of the phone is facing the other. Then ask each to describe what they see. Inevitably, one will describe a dial pad or colored array of icons and the other will describe the plain back of the phone and perhaps the logo. Then, take the side of the person whose view you see the best and ridicule the other person for their 'obviously inaccurate' perspective. Do you get the point? It's the same object but described from different perspectives. Which perspective is correct? Both! They just see the object from different points of view.

There are lots of reasons for different perspectives; gender differences and cultural differences are major. Then, enter in the uniqueness of our bodies, experiences and memories and a situation or event can be seen completely different from the way it is viewed by our spouse. Please don't get into the argument of who is right and who is wrong as it might be quite possible that both perspectives contain truth. Focus more on what an experience was like for your partner.

Some of you may be concerned that this emphasizes focus on subjective experience and minimizes the value of truth. Our experience is that truth can become clearer through discussion and sharing, especially if you explicitly ask Jesus to guide you in truth and to reveal it as you tend your relationship through respectful conversation.

We suggest using language that indicates humility, such as, *"The way I remember that situation is _____,"* or *"What I remember saying (or remember you saying) was _____, but I might be mistaken."* The key is true humility in your heart. Are you a flawed, imperfect and biased human being? Yes. We all are. Now, some have better memories than others but asserting that point isn't likely to get you very far (I know from experience). It is better to regroup in the moment with humble language to say things like, *"I don't remember saying that, or saying it like that, but I accept that is what you heard and how you heard it. So, could I try again? I want things to be good between us, so I want to be clear about what I meant."* Essentially, this type of genuine response gives wiggle room to the speaker and listener.

CHAPTER TEN | *Jeff & Jill's Marriage Tips*

Both can be 'right' and both can be 'wrong'. More importantly, for the sake of relationship, both of you will be heard, and your perspectives will be understood and honored.

Our experience has been that it's hard to refuse a polite and humble request to have an opportunity to re-explain one's experience or perspective. But the grand caveat is this: It must be truly humble. This is a significant matter for each of us to resolve in our hearts. Are we 100% accurate communicators with 100% memories? We might want to think that we are, but it is unlikely. Thus, using language to reflect the reality that we might be mistaken, or that subtle messages might leak out in our tone of voice or choice of words is humble because it reflects a heart that is willing to continue to grow per consideration of feedback from others who love us.

Tip Twelve: Fireplaces are for fires.

When was the last time your emotional brain hijacked your rational brain in a heated conversation with your spouse? What was the trigger and what fueled the fire? And what did you do to eventually work through the tangled conversation? Difficult and emotional conversations are a HUGE problem for many couples. Even happy marriages describe that 5-10% of their time is spent recovering from dark vortexes that they don't understand. And conflicted marriages often describe the primary problem as a situation that has gotten so bad that they can't talk about anything. Thus, it is imperative to have the skills and a strategy to efficiently and productively work through emotional and difficult conversations.

We won't exhaust the topic here because it's big enough that we offer a day-long seminar on the topic (and follow-up coaching for six sessions), but here is one key exercise that will help you to put your rational brain back in charge when your emotional brain has taken over.

Talk yourself through four emotions in sequence: anger, sadness, fear, gladness. First, ask for a time-out from the difficult conversation. Then ask yourself, *What am I _____ about?* Begin with mad. Answer as many times as possible until you have said everything that you realize that you are mad about. Then move to sad and do the same thing, then scared, then glad. Notice that the exercise ends on a positive emotion.[76]

This exercise will help you to gain insight into your emotions at the same time it alleviates the physical energy that accompanies the first three powerful feelings. It's like having a fireplace for a fire because it gives the fire a place to burn without burning down the house.[77] It gives you the opportunity to feel and express feelings in a way that doesn't do damage to the relationship.

After doing the exercise privately, return to the conversation with your partner. You will be calmer, more rational and insightful and articulate about your feelings.

Another way to do the exercise is with your partner. One of you takes the speaker role and the other is the listener. The listener only asks and listens. They don't reflect what the speaker says or give their opinion on what the speaker shares. They only continue to ask *"What are you* _____ *about?"* one feeling at a time. When the speaker is done with one feeling they move to the next one, eventually ending with glad feelings. One addition to this exercise that PAIRS® made was the question, *"If you were to be* _____ *about anything else, what would it be?"* after the speaker says that they don't have any more _____ feelings.[78]

Tip Thirteen: There is a difference between thoughts and feelings.

Many people get confused between thoughts and feelings. Feelings are emotions like anger, sadness, disappointment, embarrassment, fear, etc., while thoughts are conclusions based on observations, perspectives or opinions about a course of action. *"I feel that it would be good for our family to take a vacation together before our last child goes to college"* is not as accurate as saying, "I think it would be good for our family to vacation together before Laura goes to college, and I feel excited and hopeful about doing this together." Do you see the difference?

The distinction is important in our experience due to the epidemic of emotional illiteracy. *Emotional literacy is the ability to identify and express one's honest feelings, and it is a key to the bonding and attachment process in relationships.* In our experience it is common for people to struggle to identify and express their feelings.

When you share your emotions openly it increases the chances that your partner will reciprocate. You will be known, and you will get to know them regarding what is in their heart; what their most powerful emotions are attached to ... and they will know that about you too, as you continue to identify and express your emotions.

If you only talk about your thoughts, or if you talk about your feelings as if they are thoughts, you will miss the opportunities to strengthen the bond of your relationship that comes through sharing deep and powerful portions of your heart, and you won't be as likely to hear about them from others.

If this is an area you want to improve you can make a lot of progress by simply doing the exercise under the last heading, Fireplaces for Fires because it will help you to understand what you are experiencing internally. As you understand yourself better (what's inside) you can more clearly communicate to your spouse what you truly mean. And it will also help you to coach your own marriage. If you can proactively step outside of yourself and understand what you are feeling, thinking and wanting, and stop reacting to so many things (especially the negatives), you can put your best self forward to help improve the relationship.

Tip Fourteen: Distinguish between the feeling of love and the behavior of love.

Pleasure is the feeling and commitment is the behavior. Pleasure is the result of needs being met. Unfortunately, some think that this is the full extent of love and so they conclude that they have lost love in their relationship when pleasure wanes. Sadly, many couples become unwilling to continue commitment to their relationship when this happens. That's why we have focused so much on pleasure in this book and why we focus on pleasure when we coach our own marriage. It's not hard to erode it, and when good skills are used with heart and hope it isn't that hard to restore it.

We're focusing on pleasure in this chapter because in our experience the absence of pleasure in a relationship is incredibly dangerous. Mark Gungor[79] says it like this, *"You can have the best intentions for your relationship, and be mature and moral persons of faith, but if you break all the rules for relationship it isn't going to matter. It's like driving your car too fast around a corner; say 60 mph where the road is marked for 15 mph. Even if you have a fish symbol on the bumper and Christian music playing on the radio, someone is going to get hurt!"*

Our experience during seasons when there is little pleasure in our marriage is that we can still make some small progress by reminding ourselves that love is a commitment. But, we make greater progress through shared understanding of one another's thoughts, feelings and desires. Simply hearing each other's hearts with good-will and skill quickly lessens the pain, and begins the restoration of peace and pleasure. Time after time we have personally experienced and witnessed in others that it only takes a spark of hope to get the fire going again.

A Concluding Encouragement

Grand tours in bicycle racing (e.g., Tour de France; a total of nearly 3000 miles) are about four weeks long. Riders race nearly every day for 100-150 miles and then get up the next day and do it again. Most racers aren't selected for these events until they're about ten years into their racing career (mid-twenties for most). Why? It takes years of conditioning and learning to be prepared for rigors of intense competition every day for a month. They must have a lot of training miles in their legs, and be able to recover quickly without falling victim to fatigue, illness, overuse injuries or mental fatigue that could result in potentially fatal crashes at anywhere from 25-70 mph! Grand Tours are incredibly difficult and only the fittest and best prepared athletes compete for victory, let alone finish the race which many consider a victory in itself.

What's the point of comparing Grand Tours to marriage? For a marriage to thrive over time, let alone survive, requires ongoing acquisition of knowledge and skills for the journey. Participants are never done learning and never done applying all they've learned to lovingly communicate, respectfully resolve conflict and to live to fight another day. Couples that have good to great marriages over decades testify that it hasn't always been smooth, and that they've fallen down a few times, but that time after time they got back up, regrouped and tried again, just as racers who fall off their bikes and get back up to rejoin the race with hope, heart and skill.

CHAPTER TEN
Reflection Questions:

1. Which tip would your marriage say would be most helpful?

_____

_____

_____

_____

_____

2. Which tip do you most want to use in your relationship?

_____

_____

_____

_____

_____

3. Which tip would your spouse say is most helpful?

_____

_____

_____

_____

_____

CHAPTER ELEVEN

A Marriage Built for Others

When God initiates healing and growth it isn't just for us, but also for others. His purpose in blessing us is that we might be a blessing. What you receive from God for your marriage is for you AND for others: your children, their children, your family, friends, and the Church. God wants to display His power to heal and to strengthen your marriage and then to use your testimony to inspire other marriages to trust Him to do the same for them.

This is God's economy throughout history. He gives so that we might give to others. But there's an inherent danger in this formula that many miss. *If we don't give to others we might lose what we've been given.* Or, stated in more positive way, we *keep what we have and increase it through giving.* This reality is reflected in the common cliché, *"You can't out give God,"* and notably in a maxim oft repeated in twelve-step recovery groups, "You keep your sobriety by giving what you have learned and received to others; help others get sober and you will continue in sobriety yourself".

The following stories are real-life examples of miraculous restoration and faithful and generous giving to others that we hope will inspire you to do likewise.

From the Brink to the Boardroom

Porter and Joanie Shellhammer came to our marriage mentoring training event[80] as a last ditch effort to save their marriage. They thought it was a seminar that targeted couples having struggles, so when they learned that it was actually a training event they were tempted to leave. But, they decided to stay because of something that intrigued them. As presenters, we shared openly about our own marriage; the warts, the wrinkles, the conflicts and struggles as well as some victories. They later reported that the effect of such openness was inspirational,

155

"We said to each other, 'As trainers they're more open about their marriage publicly in front of all these people than we are privately with each other. If they can do that publicly, perhaps we can try the same in private.'"

Thankfully, couples in the seminar were given the opportunity to practice skills and to do exercises on site. Our presentation format was to teach a concept, model a skill and exercise, then break for couples to have 15-20 minutes to practice on their own. This allowed them to experience some success in sharing honest thoughts, feelings and desires with each other in a way that gave them hope for their future!

Three months later I saw the Shellhammers at a community marriage event in Tallahassee, Florida. Their enthusiasm was over the top! *"What you and Jill did at that seminar this summer saved our marriage!"* What? I had to hear more. It was then I learned the effect of transparent sharing by us in the seminar. *"You didn't act as if you had it all together, but rather let us look into the real stuff of your lives and how the concepts, skills and exercises you shared that helped you to work through challenges in your marriage. That encouraged us to try to communicate differently, and as we have success doing that we have more and more hope, and pleasure in our relationship again."*

I'll never forget the late night conversation Porter and I had that evening. He shared a dream to share the victories he and Joanie were winning with colleagues in the fire service, and with any other couple with whom they could gain audience. Why? Because they were yet another couple who'd been to hell in their relationship, and knew that it was possible to recover to the point of thriving in pleasure and purpose. That's a story they yearned to tell.

The rest of the story is that six years later, Porter and Joanie are established in full-time marriage ministry serving as regional directors of a national marriage ministry, board members of a local marriage resource center, and founding directors of their own ministry to couples. Their marriage is a superb example of a marriage revived and built for others, serving generously and faithfully to bless others as they've been blessed.

Reconciled for Others

Rich and Sharon are another incredible story. Theirs was a marriage void of pleasure for years. Richard was morose and Sharon was angry, and it was a vicious cycle in which they went round and round until she snapped. In August 2003 with the support of her pastor, she asked Rich to leave. She was done with negativity and a lack of success communicating and resolving differences.

I (Jeff) received the call as a counselor recommended by the pastor. Soon I was involved in one of the most difficult cases I'd ever encountered. Their marriage hung in the balance for a long season of counseling (18 months) but throughout, both were consistently willing to submit to the Lordship of Jesus Christ. Many times each of them expressed their desire to stop trying, but they didn't have release from God to quit and so they persisted. Thus, it was ultimately God who held them together.

Significant progress toward reconciliation came for Rich through a coaching approach to understanding his thoughts, feelings, desires and dreams. And state of the art relationship skills that work well as part of the coaching approach helped him to develop compassion for Sharon and how she experienced their marriage. For Sharon, it was unreasonable hope in faith that Rich could change that helped her to persist. Thus, it was a combination of state of the art relationship skills and exercises used with heart that strengthened her heart and helped to heal their marriage.

One of the highlights of my career as a people helper was January 1, 2005 as a co-facilitator for a public reconciliation ceremony in which Rich and Sharon renewed their marriage vows. The Wildman's marriage had been given a miracle, and they cooperated with it through continued willingness to hope in faith for God's best as they also used effective skills and exercises to share and work through a multitude of issues.

Today they too are engaged in marriage ministry, and they continue to manage their family farm as a team of two. They've been through Marriage Coaching training and today they coach couples together and both meet with men and women individually who are separated and ambivalent about or opposed to reconciliation. Their message is one of unreasonable hope and perseverance, and their ministry is appropriately entitled, Stubborn Pursuits![81]

How Helping Marriages Helps Your Marriage

When we chat with either of these couples today we often reflect on what God has done in their marriages, and how they are stewards of the marriage miracles they've been given. One thing is always clear: *They stay fresh in their own marriage by helping other couples.* The same is true for us. Helping others is one of the most enjoyable and rewarding things we do. Why? How does this work?

First, we think it is the blessing of God on a couple willing to live for others and not just themselves. He continues to pour knowledge, grace and pleasure into marriages dedicated to serving Him by serving other brides and bridegrooms.

Second, serving other couples keeps ideas, skills and exercises fresh in our own minds. In order to genuinely and effectively model for other couples, couples who help other couples must use what they teach and practice what they preach. It's very compelling to a couple we're coaching when we say, *"We just used this skill or exercise this morning!"* You can see the surprised look in their eyes when we dare to be so transparent and personal. They often say, *"Your openness about your own marriage made the difference for us. We said, 'If they can do that, we can to.'"*

Third, the sacred responsibility of serving other marriages keeps us accountable to keep working on our own marriage. We realize that private victory is the birthplace of public credibility, and that we don't have any authority or effectiveness in the lives of others except for that which we have won in our own lives. Who we are is what we have to give, and so who we are, and how we relate in love, with hope and through good skills must always be in process in our private life.

It's Not All Roses

But we don't want to delude you that once you accrue a critical mass of skills and understanding to help your own marriage and to help others that life will be happy ever after! The truth is that if things go as well as possible, they won't be smooth. Part of this is due to the fact that we're humans living in an ever changing and challenging world. The other part is the specialized ongoing preparation process orchestrated by God Himself to ensure that we experience and learn what He wants us to impart to others.

The reality for marriages that serve other marriages is that we are sometimes attacked by the enemy. It's uncanny how often before public events to teach about marriage, or even just before a critical marriage coaching session we experience conflict and tension. We'll have difficulty communicating, experience a misunderstanding or one of us will become impatient. These kinds of things have happened to us and other couples often enough that we now believe that Satan is sometimes behind the problem; that he sends his demonic minions to harass us at strategic times that could distract us (at a minimum) or nullify the potential effectiveness of our upcoming ministry opportunity. Obviously, this makes it imperative to be girded with the full armor of God (Ephesians 6), and to be protected through personal diligence in spiritual disciplines and the protection of intercessory prayer of Christian brothers and sisters.

We hope this serves as a sober reminder to you and doesn't scare you away from ministering to others. Just know that it is very serious business to be proactive in spiritual protection of your relationship. Tragically we've trained some couples that had great ambition, but were defeated by the enemy and are now divorced. Hindsight revealed that they either had hidden issues that they hadn't been willing to address or that they didn't take proactive nurturing and protection of their marriage seriously enough.

God's Plan for Godly Marriages

A godly marriage serves God's purposes while also providing joy, pleasure and fulfillment for a couple. It is a relationship that reflects the relationship of the Bridegroom Jesus and His Bride, the Church. It is also a relationship in which we are able to experience God's pleasure.

Fulfilling some of the desires of your partner's heart is a good aim in marriage, but not the sole aim and not the overarching purpose of the relationship. Still, the fulfillment of desires is a powerful God-given motivator and driver of behavior, and great marriage insurance. It is human nature that when we experience the feelings of love and pleasure, we are likely to continue to do those things. And when both partners do these things for each other it keeps the relationship healthy and strong. Some of the world's happiest and most fulfilled people are those that make their life about others. How can you do this with what you've learned?

The famous psychiatrist Milton Erickson understood the paradoxical principle of finding life by giving oneself away. He illustrates this well through a story about his treatment of a chronically depressed woman.[82] After assessing her condition, his prescription was for her to buy a dozen flowers a day for two weeks. Each day she was to give the flowers away, one at a time, to someone that she deemed to be in need of some cheer!

After two weeks she had her next appointment with the unorthodox psychiatrist. When asked about her depression she reported that it had vanished. How? You guessed it. She'd lost sight of herself and her troubles by focusing on the needs of others. Her mood lifted each time she gave a flower to a cheerless soul. Sometimes they smiled and replied with gratitude, but at the very least, she felt satisfaction from exercising loving kindness. A lot of people ended up being helped by a depressed psychiatric patient. What a wonder! Could giving your marriage to others immunize it to negativity and depression?

What One Couple Can Do, Another Can Do

Through many personal trials involving career, family and friendships, Jill and I have continued to serve marriages. Sometimes the positive progress and outcomes for others has been our greatest joy in the context of personal tribulation and heartache.

You may wonder if we had any business helping others while we ourselves were suffering. Certainly not if we had been so compromised that we couldn't function in a professional manner or avoid bringing our personal struggles into the spotlight in a way that dominated our sessions, but neither was the case. Instead, we checked our issues at the door, unless modeling a skill or exercise required transparent sharing. It was then that we opened the reality of our lives to others, effectively boasting of our weakness in order that the power of Christ would rest on us,[83] and the effectiveness of our good-hearted use of a coaching process to coach our own marriage would be clear.

Our transparency in those moments, and dedication to teaching skills and facilitating couples to conduct life-giving conversations has been good for them AND good for us! What we've done, you can do! Please do this. Others are waiting to receive what God has given (and will give) to you. It will be good for them, good for you, and good for God's Kingdom!

CHAPTER ELEVEN
Reflection Questions:

1. What is exciting and inspiring to you about possibly experiencing good things in your marriage as a result of serving others?

_____

_____

_____

_____

_____

2. What have you been thinking about doing to protect your marriage?

_____

_____

_____

_____

_____

3. What are your thoughts about God's desires and plans for godly marriages?

_____

_____

_____

_____

_____

A Recipe for Your Marriage

In chapter four we compared the ingredients needed in marriage coaching to a bread recipe. My mom used to make a wonderful sourdough to die for and my mouth is beginning to water as I type. Now, think one more time about those ingredients of bread and the varying quantities needed to produce this magnificent food: water, flour, yeast, salt and eggs. When all of the necessary ingredients are mixed and baked the result is delicious! The same is true for marriage. Combining essential ingredients on a regular basis produces a healthy and pleasurable relationship!

The essential ingredients we presented earlier were heart, hope, and skills. Then we presented the core skills of marriage coaching. Now, it's up to you how to combine the ingredients and the skills. You've been shown around the kitchen. You know where the ingredients are and how to find the utensils to mix them and cook them. You have the basics of what you need to make the dishes that your marriage needs. Now, just like when you learned to cook, you need to go through the experience of trial and error of adjusting recipes and cooking your concoctions to the taste that your marriage is asking for.

Basically, we want to encourage you to continually evaluate and adjust your recipe according to what your marriage needs at any given time. Whenever there is absence of pleasure or your marriage is in conflict and pain, it is a good time to step back to review the recipe you've been using. Sometimes you'll simply want to edify your relationship. Ask your marriage how your current recipe is working and if there is any adjustment needed. It's like sampling soup and then deciding what to add. For Jill and me it's during seasons of diminished pleasure or the presence of pain that we examine our ingredients and adjust our recipes.

Here is one of our recent conversations.

"We've not understood each other very well lately. We seem to be having a hard time getting on the same page," Jill said.

"Yeah, I think if our marriage could make a request it would be for a long uninterrupted conversation during which we could both share our honest feelings about some recent family experiences, as well as our individual task lists and upcoming schedule," I said.

"Well, let's try that then. When would be a good time and for how long?" Jill asked.

"Let's walk that three mile loop later this morning, and see how far we get in conversation while walking," I suggested.

Do you see what happened? We realized a problem: disconnected understanding. The first step was to ask our marriage what it needed. As we both contributed to the conversation we agreed on a solution: time to talk. In our marriage, walking and talking works for us. Thus, the answer came from a pantry of proven solutions. By the way, when we talked, we made sure to ask and listen with heart and skill! It worked! We reconnected, and gained confidence in our ability to troubleshoot challenges in our relationship. If it hadn't worked we would have gone back to the drawing board to brainstorm another possible solution. Note too that it didn't take very long to come up with a solution. The more you practice this process the more efficient you will become.

Now, you try it:
1. Name the problem.
2. Ask your marriage to talk to you. *"What do you want/need?"*
3. Collaborate about some possible solutions.
4. Evaluate the outcome.

YOUR recipe for a healthy, strong and pleasurable marriage will be unique, but it is likely to include frequent use of skills to open and hold each other's hearts, to set shared goals and to resolve conflict in a way that builds your relationship. Take stock. What new tools and exercises do you have in your toolbox since you have been practicing skills we covered in earlier chapters? Anything from this book and other resources that has ever been helpful to your marriage is part of the stock in your pantry from which you can choose to create a recipe for your marriage.

Ingredients in Jeff and Jill's Marriage Recipe

Our marriage needs the following:
1. Time to talk
2. Physical affection
3. Shared goals to work on together
4. Boundaries between work and personal (recreation and rejuvenation)
5. Walks
6. Travel together
7. Prayer

When we have disagreements we can usually track the beginning of tension or disconnectedness to a period of time when we neglected the essential ingredients for sustainable pleasure in our relationship. The fix is often to simply reinsert those ingredients. A coaching approach is well suited to help your marriage to quickly assess what is lacking and to make a plan for good relational nutrition.

Here's another example of a recipe for success. Think about what you eat. Which foods make you feel great? You probably know by experimentation or accidental discovery which foods give you strength, mental sharpness, etc. For instance if I want to be super strong on a bicycle ride of 35-50 miles, I've found that a meal that includes salmon, pasta, bread and salad for dinner the night before the ride does the trick. On the other hand, if I need to be really sharp all afternoon for work, then a lunch of salad, a chicken breast and iced tea is the perfect combination. If I simply want my tummy to be happy (temporarily) then a quart of mint chocolate chip ice cream is the ticket! You get the point.

Now apply this process of identifying essential ingredients for your marriage. What has worked for you in the past? Certainly you've conducted your own little scientific experiments by noting the ingredients or recipe that produced good results in different areas of your life. Use the same process to observe your marriage and then work together to choose the ingredients to accomplish your goal.

How to Know You're Ready to Coach Your Marriage

Couples we have coached know that they are ready to end a season of Marriage Coaching, and to begin coaching their own marriage, when they are confident in their ability to use new skills on their own. The pleasure in their marriage has increased substantially, and they have clear ideas about what they need to do and how often they need to do it in order to function at an optimum level. In other words, they know the ingredients of the recipe they need to sustain and protect their marriage, and they know how to combine them. When you coach your own marriage, you know that you have a great recipe by a high overall rating of pleasure in the relationship which usually corresponds with the degree to which your needs are being met.[84]

Recipes vary from couple to couple. Most contain the same ingredients, but quantities vary. Still, the principle is the same. Diligence in following a recipe for success is a great way to protect your relationship.

Common Marriage Recipe Ingredients:
1. Communication about daily activities
2. Sharing of new information and emerging desires
3. Conversations to resolve conflict in a way that builds the relationship

4. Affection and intimacy
5. Recreation and fun
6. Prayer

Many couples we've coached experience vast improvement in closeness and pleasure by simply doing a 10-15 minute conversational exercise every day (See Appendix F). That says something about the helpfulness of the exercise, but also about how much good can be accomplished in relationship by being intentional and disciplined about having consistent, quality conversations!

Applying What You've Learned

You can have a well-stocked pantry, refrigerator, freezer and spice cabinet but until you do the work of combining the ingredients according to your favorite recipes you won't have a meal to eat. And if you go long enough without eating, you'll starve. Sadly, that's what we hear from emaciated marriages in our counseling practice, *"We knew we were growing apart, but we didn't make time to work on our relationship."* From our perspective this is tragic because there are plenty of state of the art ingredients and information available for the couple that will take time to shop and then to learn how to cook. The reality is that the cache of information and skills you need to heal, strengthen and protect your marriage is right around the corner; it's at your fingertips on the internet; it's in this book!

Unnecessary pain in relationships and forever fractured relationships is the one big problem in the world that makes us want to beat our fist on the table in frustration to say, *"It doesn't have to be this way!"* You don't have to starve due to lack of essential ingredients to make your marriage what you want it to be and what God wants it to be. But you do have to learn to cook. That takes time and effort but the results are worth it.

Getting Practical

We want to end this book with crystal clear directions to make an effective recipe for your marriage. Begin by reflecting on a time when things were good (at least better than now). When was your relationship pleasurable? What was happening when things felt good between you? What did you experience with each other? Common answers include: *"We talked a lot. We did things together. We had shared dreams that we worked on together."* Rate your experience in that season of your marriage on a scale of 1-10, with 10 being great and one being poor, and then estimate where you are now in comparison.

Maybe the "happy" period was a nine and your rating now is a five. What was happening in your marriage when it was a nine and what is happening currently at a five? What would you like to happen more or to start happening that would let you say six, seven, or eight? Answers to that question can provide potential action-steps and strategies to build and sustain pleasure in your relationship! Specifically, what skills and exercises have you learned in previous chapters that might help you to accomplish a higher rating?

Here's another example from our recent past. While living on the East Coast (U.S.), we regularly walked and talked—near daily walks of an hour or so were common. We were definitely spoiled to have that much time to invest in us. Our schedules simply made it possible to be together a lot during that season of life. Our walks were a time when we focused only on us; not the kids, the phone, the computers, etc. We had ample time to share feelings, ideas and desires. It was a time we looked forward to, and we got used to it. This was a habit for the better part of four years. Then we moved and our schedules and responsibilities changed, walks and talks became less frequent. We started to feel disconnected, so we asked why, and rated the pleasure in our relationship as compared to the past?

That was a great opportunity to coach our own marriage. We felt disconnected so we took a step back to ask our marriage to speak to us. *"If our marriage could make a request, what would it ask for?"* The answer was simple and clear. *"It would ask us to walk together more often,"* was the answer that came to both of our minds. Next was to figure out when to walk and talk. In addition, for us, prayer is also involved in these conversations. This is another great way to coach your own marriage, to ask The Great Physician and The Wonderful Counselor to speak to you about your marriage. *"Lord, what would you have us to understand about our relationship right now? Why are we feeling less pleasure and less connection, and what can we do about it?"*

Once you have answers to these questions, work yourselves through the process of developing action-steps. Generate a list of things you could do, then evaluate those according to effectiveness and desirability (i.e., "Which ones do we want to do, and which ones do we think will work?"). Finally, commit to one or more action-steps by deciding duration and date(s) that you will do it. For example our action-strategy for walking is 30 minutes/day on weekdays, and one hour or more each day on the weekends.

Your Unique Recipe

Take a few minutes to think about the recipe for your relationship. Ask God to give you memory about effective ingredients from the past and your desires in the present. Step back from your relationship to ask your marriage to speak to you. *"If you could speak, what would you (my marriage) ask for?"*

Jill and I have two distinct memories of great times for our marriage on vacation. The setting was lovely, (Anna Maria Island, Florida), but it was the relaxed communication and sharing of days together that were the highlight: food, sleep, affection and fun. Now we know that vacation isn't reality, but there was something to be learned that could be applied at home, to an extent. We can be intentional about sharing preparation of meals. We can prioritize and set limits and boundaries around sleep and rest, and we can make time for affection and fun. Of course day to day life isn't like vacation, but with a little work on our schedules, we can include vacation ingredients in daily life.

Think back to a time things were great, no matter when or where. Don't succumb to the temptation to evaluate the ingredients from that period as unrealistic. Dreaming in faith is daring to hope for that which you don't yet see or realize. But, you have an advocate in the One who ordained marriage to work on your behalf to make it everything you would like it to be and what He wants it to be.

Here's the kind of conversation we have with God pretty regularly, *"Lord, you told us in the Gospel of John that the thief comes to steal, to kill and to destroy, but that you have come that we might have life abundantly. We want your abundance in marriage. We want the fullness of pleasure, joy, hope and purpose that you created us to live. Not just for our own sake, but that these might flow through us to others so that they too might enjoy the abundance you intend. Please give us creative ideas about the ingredients and recipe we need to experience what you want us to have. In Jesus' name. Amen."*

CHAPTER TWELVE
Reflection Questions:

1. Do you have a recipe for your marriage yet? If not, what could you do to determine the ingredients and how to combine them?

_____

_____

_____

_____

2. Which ingredients mentioned in this chapter are ones that are definitely part of the unique recipe for your marriage? Have you identified any other ingredients that weren't mentioned?

_____

_____

_____

_____

_____

3. Where in your daily, weekly, monthly schedule will you make time to use the recipe that you have discerned for your marriage?

_____

_____

_____

_____

Final Words

Hopefully you have found a nugget or two in this book that will make a difference in your marriage. Our greatest hope is that you will try. Try to use some of the skills. Try the exercises. Persist in the development of a Christ-like heart, and dare God to give you His imagination for what He wants your marriage to be. Avoid doing nothing, because you can't do everything. Do what you can. The results may surprise you.

What will it take to have the marriage you dream about and that God wants you to have? It will probably require hard work on an ongoing basis, but it's not something you have to do alone. You can connect with other couples on the journey, and you have the Holy Spirit to provide supernatural strength and determination to do well one day at a time.

Believe us about our own marriage and the ones we've shared about. At one point or another many of us thought that we might be past the point of recovery due to too much history, too much pain and not enough willingness or ability in ourselves or our partners to grow and change. But God met us at our point of weakness to give us what only He could give; the ability to hope in faith, to love and try with His heart, and to experience a different quality of relating through proven skills and effective processes. *What one couple can do, another couple can do!*

Your marriage may not be in dire straits, but don't be deluded that it will always be free of strife. Your best defense is a good offense. Prevent misunderstandings, build closeness and steward the pleasure you have by nurturing it with loving listening, curious asking and effective goal-settings. Reach for all that God has for you to enjoy in your matrimony even as you continually ask Him to guide you about how to share it with others.

Please put this book to use. Read it and re-read it to the point that you dog ear the pages. Follow the sequence of steps to coach your own marriage and to set shared goals. And don't just read. Put the recommended steps into action! Ask your marriage what it wants and what it needs. Envision the ideal future of your marriage; what God wants you to have, who He wants you to be, what He wants you to experience and what He wants you to do. Ask Him to help you to heal your relationship, and then honor the desires of the heart of your marriage by coaching it. And please share your testimonies, ask for help, and give to and bless others as you are blessed and as you learn and grow!

To God is the Glory!

With hope and love,
Jeff and Jill Williams

BONUS CHAPTER

Crisis Management

Chances are 50/50 that if you bought this book it's because there is some pain in your marriage or a marriage you care about; perhaps even a crisis. We suspect this because of the number of couples in crisis who sign up for marriage enrichment events even when the advertisement says, "Not for couples in crisis".

We respect that if your marriage is in crisis you probably don't have time or patience to read the whole book for ideas of what to do because a relationship crisis is the equivalent of discovering that your house is on fire during the middle of the night. The main objective is to survive the fire not to clean up or improve the house. That comes later after the fire is out and the occupants are safe. After the crisis has passed is a much better time to absorb the principles and skills of marriage coaching to heal, strengthen and protect your marriage; after the fire of crisis is out and you're no longer panicked about simply surviving.[85]

Let's quickly review some signs of crisis and then we'll get into some key actions and attitudes for your response to it. Then in the last part of the chapter we'll focus on some of the keys to recovery.

Indicators that your marriage is in crisis!

If your marriage is in crisis, some of these signs might be present: You might feel shocked, devastated and hopeless. You may alternate between feeling numb and furious. You might have episodes of sobbing or you can't stop crying. It feels like a bomb just went off in your life and you feel shattered, broken and possibly feel there is no hope for recovery. You're not sure what to do and you want to find some help. One or more of the following has happened to you:

- You just learned about something that threatens your marriage (e.g., that your spouse has been having an affair or other secrets like an addiction, financial dishonesty, etc.).
- You're feeling some degree of hopelessness and/or pain.
  - You don't feel loved and you don't feel loving.
- Your partner has said some things that you can't imagine recovering from:
  - I want a divorce.
  - Our marriage was a mistake.
  - I've never loved you or I don't love you anymore.
  - I'll never be enough for you.
  - You'll never be what I need, and you'll never change.
  - I don't love you anymore.
- You're so fed up that you've been having serious fantasies about quitting and leaving the relationship and having a different life altogether.
  - You think life might be better with someone else.
- You've considered some steps you would need to take for a different life:
  - Hiding and/or saving money.
  - Seeking legal counsel.
  - Making secret arrangements to live somewhere else.
  - Seeing a counselor and not telling your spouse.

Do these sound familiar? FYI, it takes one to know one. We know how awful and how hopeless things can feel. We know the feelings of desperation to get out of and away from the pain and the pleasure of fantasies about a different life. At its raw core, this book is our testimony about the times it felt like our marriage was dying and what we did in cooperation with God's plan to resurrect us.

What follows in this chapter are some of the actions we did and some of the attitudes we adopted that contributed to restoration. Thankfully we are thriving again to the extent that we enjoy the daily blessing of ministering to other couples with all that God has given to us.

Two critical factors in crisis are attitudes and actions. The attitudes you adopt affect your perspective, feelings and actions. And your actions make the critical difference between whether or not your marriage will survive AND the extent to which it will recover and thrive in the future. Attitude is the way you think about the situation that affects your feelings and actions are the things you do that will either contribute to restoration or the demise of your marriage.

Crisis = A Dangerous Opportunity

The first thing to remember is that a crisis is a dangerous opportunity. These are the two symbols in the Chinese language used to form the word crisis, 'danger' and 'opportunity'. It is real that your marriage could die, be wounded or maimed beyond repair. Perhaps you're thinking, *It already has*. Hang on. Hear us out. It is also possible that through this crisis your marriage could be rescued and restored. Remarkably, some couples eventually claim that their crisis was the best thing that ever happened to their marriage because it forced them to get really honest with each other and to be intentional about developing a robust and healthy relationship!

Think about the dangerous opportunity of a health crisis. Perhaps you've been through one and the outcome didn't look very good. The ultimate danger is death. The opportunity is restoration to complete health, and perhaps a wake-up call to the importance of exercise and nutrition to restore and protect health as well as renewed perspective about the preciousness of life. We know people that say a heart attack, skin cancer or other health crisis was the best thing that happened to them to provide a reality check on their lifestyle and a wake-up call to the things (and people) in life that really matter.

Just last year Jill and I had some moments when we wondered if she was on her way to Heaven. It was June 2010 when she was hospitalized with a life-threatening infection. Without medical intervention it is certain that she would have died, but with proper care she was completely healed. Today she has no remnants of lasting problems from that illness. And both of our perspectives about the preciousness of life and what's really important is forever changed! Things that used to worry us simply don't matter anymore. At least we're both alive and together to enjoy life's challenges!

If your marriage is in crisis it could die, or you could take the steps to restore and renew it as well as to protect it from more danger in the future. Again, we say 'hang on' because we've talked with enough couples to predict your next response, *You don't know how bad it is. I'm done, and even if God wants to give us a miracle, I'm not sure that I'll be willing to receive it.* We urge you to hang on with a hopeful attitude because we've heard things like this from quite a few marriages that have survived to thrive.

In the Middle of the Crisis?

Hang On!

Don't quit, there's hope! While your enemy, the devil is relentlessly attempting to destroy you, there's help available from heaven on earth. God has imparted gifts and knowledge to some of His servants so that your marriage can be saved, healed and protected for His purposes.

Don't let the enemy have his way! Don't let him win! Recognize that all hopeless thoughts and feelings are ones that he is planting or nurturing so that you will take action to kill your marriage. Don't do it. Many a couple has lived to regret impulsive behaviors that further hurt their relationship; such as revenge affairs, angry words, even Facebook messages! Take wisdom from the Bible which points out that you can't retrieve spoken words any more easily than you can retrieve an arrow that's been launched from its bow!

Conversely, recognize that hope in faith springs from God Himself. And, please consider in the midst of your desperate pain that He is the one who can do "immeasurably more than we can ask for or imagine." No matter the depth of your pain and all the water that has gone under the bridge in your marriage, please allow a little bit of doubt to seep into your mind and heart. Your marriage may be in the process of a miracle, even if it doesn't feel like it. In fact, let us ask you this, *"If God wants to give you a miracle for your marriage, would you be willing to receive it?"*

Putting a Fire in its Place

Crisis in marriage is like a fire that gets out of the fireplace. A coal from a log pops out onto the carpet or a pile of papers or kindling. You've only got a few seconds to put it out (or put the coal back into the fireplace) before it ignites something flammable and you have a problem that's out of control. Similarly, when passions burn hot in marriage things are said and done that are like the coal that pops out of place. Things ignite and begin to burn. Just as your response to a house fire would be first to handle it and then to get out if it got out of control, you may be tempted to quickly run from the dangerous and painful flames of the fire in your relationship. But you might stay to fight the fire if you know how to do it and you have the right equipment.

Think about how to handle a fire. If you catch it in time a big disaster can be avoided. Do you have fire extinguishers or sprinklers in your home? Have you practiced using them so that you can quickly and skillfully react if it happens? While working for a public agency I received training with several extinguishers. Ever since I've been more confident that I could possibly extinguish a fire before it gets out of control. If you've been trained then you know what I mean. Chances are that you would be fairly rational and calm if, for instance, a grease fire started in the kitchen and you had an appropriate extinguisher close by. You would certainly experience adrenaline, but your first instinct to run from danger could be overcome by the realization that you have a tool that you know how to use to help to handle the problem. Training to use the proper tool would increase the chances that you would stay in the situation rather than running from it.

So it is with marriage. If you have tools to use to handle hot and dangerous times in your relationship you can stay to douse the flames rather than running from them. *"That's great theory Jeff, but we don't have any tools, and we don't know what to do!"* Hang on, we'll get there.

Slow Down

There's a lot riding on your decisions about your marriage. In fact, so much depends on what you decide now that it deserves ample time to think about it. Give yourself at least 6-8 weeks before you make any final decisions. In the meantime, secure competent and effective coaching and/or counseling to help you to work through your emotions, rationally analyze your situation, and to understand how every aspect of your life—including all of your relationships—will be affected if you end your marriage.

Like many instances of death by suicide, the impulsive death of a marriage comes when a person feels completely hopeless and without options to solve problems and pain. They just want it to end, and don't have much energy or desire to consider the consequences. They are desperate for the pain to end and they rationalize it like this, *Even if my decision causes pain, it won't be as much pain as what I'm experiencing now*, or *The pleasurable result of my choice (e.g., physical death, or being alone or with a different person) is worth the pain that I and others might go through as a result of my choice.* But neither is true. There are simply too many testimonies from persons who have lived to regret their decisions to believe otherwise. This is not to say that there aren't any circumstances in which divorce is healthy and best (e.g., domestic violence, unfaithfulness, and other unhealthy situations).[86] Still, in crisis it is easy to rationalize a slippery path to divorce instead of waiting for more rational and clear thinking to prevail.

The person who commits suicide does not have a clear picture and appreciation for the vast quantities of enduring emotional pain they will cause to others. Similarly, the person who impulsively ends their marriage often fails to accurately estimate and appreciate the depth of grief and the extended duration of the pain that can result for them and for others affected by their decision (spouse, children, parents, friends, etc.).[87]

Just as death by suicide is a permanent solution for a temporary problem, so is the decision to end marriage. People do both because no solutions are apparent, but that is the crux of the intervention; to buy time for hopelessness to recede and solutions to emerge. Give yourself ample time to consider your options. You don't have to make a decision as quickly as the crisis came upon you.

Stop the Bleeding

Soldiers rescue wounded comrades from the line of fire so that they don't receive more injuries. Remove yourself from the conversation (or verbal fight). Go to another room, or leave the house to go somewhere safe (friend, family, etc.). Don't expose yourself to further injury and don't injure your partner with anymore impulsive words or actions. Your marriage is already wounded and in danger of dying. Don't risk another, potentially fatal wound.

Some couples need a period of separation that gives them time to de-escalate emotions and to take an objective look at the relationship from a different perspective (more on this, just below). Couples can become so caught up participating in the relationship that they miss the opportunity to take a step back to observe it. It's the difference between being a player on the field or a spectator in the grandstands. Making some space between you can provide desperately needed peace and rest, and prevent further injury to each other.

But whether you continue to live in the same home or separate we advise you to be very careful with any and all verbal exchanges. The maxim that many of us learned in kindergarten applies: If you can't say something nice, don't say anything. Applied to marriage, we say it this way. "As you endeavor to stop hurting each other and to begin the healing process, be sure to use good skills with good heart."

As the Crisis Wanes but Problems Remain

It's not that the crisis isn't a crisis anymore, but after a few days or weeks the shock wears off a bit, emotions aren't as strong or disabling, but there's still a problem that needs to be dealt with. As a potential casualty you got out of the house before the fire took your life, and you've received first aid. Your wounds are bandaged but not healed. Just as you would cautiously and slowly approach the scene of a house fire or a bombing to view the damage and perhaps to recover valued possessions, it is essential that you proceed slowly and skillfully to assess the state of your relationship and what can be done about it.

Two Types of Separation: Sudden and Strategic

Sometimes a period of separation is needed to save a marriage. Often it happens immediately after one spouse discovers a devastating secret such as an affair or secret gambling with the children's college tuition money and the offended spouse can't stand to be in the same house with the betrayer. *"Get out"* they scream! So it's off to the house of a friend, parent or sibling for an unspecified period of time.

The other type of separation is planned and strategic. Sometimes we even suggest it as a way to move forward because a couple has made it clear that continuing to live together is doing more harm than good and/or they desperately need some silence and solitude to think clearly about the situation; what they want, what God wants, and a strategy to attempt to repair the relationship.

The Benefits of a Separation[88]

Whether reactive or planned, separation is absolutely necessary for some couples. It may last anywhere from a few days to a few months, according to the unique circumstances of the marriage and the criteria the couple establishes to come back together. While it poses some risks,[89] it can be effective to stop the hurting. Ultimately, separation is for marriages that are at risk of dying if either partner receives one more blow from the other and/or they aren't going to go forward unless and until one or both embraces the opportunity for deep healing and restoration.

Stopping the hurting is really hard and counter-intuitive for some temperaments. Some of us intense, strong-willed problem-solvers pursue our partners with determination to "solve" the problem by saying a few more things that we believe will get them to see things our way, get them to apologize, etc. Unfortunately it is conversations like these that are sometimes the final straw for spouses that need time and space to process things and to recover from upsetting conversations.

Sadly, we've heard statements like this way too many times: *"He just doesn't know when to stop! He has no idea how much damage he did, and now I'm kicking myself for giving him another chance. He just proved that he isn't going to change."* Tragically, that's been the last thing we hear from some spouses before they tell us they're going ahead with divorce. It would have been so much better, marriage-saving in fact, for them to have separated before the coup de grace was applied to the marriage.

Do your marriage a favor. Stop the hurting and get help to have healing conversations. If it takes a separation to facilitate this don't be afraid of it. Simply structure the separation for a set period of time with a specific plan for the times you will come together to work on the relationship; at first with a counselor or Marriage Coaching couple, and then on your own as a couple as you gain confidence in skills and exercises to help you have productive and healing conversations.[90] Do everything you can to get the skills you need and the help you need to interact in a way that will promote healing and to develop a heart of humility, compassion and selflessness so that your words and actions will flow from a clean and loving heart. If you don't, you may not have a marriage to worry about. If it takes a separation to accomplish a greater good then do it. It may seem like you're going backwards, but it really can be a case of going backward to go forward.

In my practice as a counselor I've served numerous couples who lived separately for months, and only talked to each other in my office with me serving as facilitator and mediator to structure and referee their conversations. This has been really hard for couples who were used to a lot more interaction, but in many cases it worked to heal the relationship. Often, a few decent conversations conducted with good heart and skill fan the smoldering embers of a relationship to life. Don't think that the fire of your relationship will begin to burn bright and hot right away, but at least it won't die, and while the fire comes back to life, both of you will see and feel the potential for your relationship to live, and it's a whole lot less likely that it will turn into a fire that burns down the house!

A final benefit of a strategic separation is to create an "as if" scenario. Temporary separation, with desire/intent to reconcile, provides an opportunity to both partners to experience what it might be like to live life without each other in the future. While some couples report immediate relief by having a private sanctuary to recover, many eventually report that they don't like it; that they didn't know what they had until it was gone, and that they want to do whatever it takes in themselves and with their partner to make things right. Again, the period of separation should include some facilitated conversations to spark hope for healing and a future together and not a bridge that moves one of the partners away from the relationship for good.

Secure Expert Counsel

Who do you know that is experienced in situations like this, and who do you trust? Friends and family are often the first groups of people that you'll think of, but while they care about you, they may not be rational and objective and they may not have experience or helpful counsel to offer. More times than I care to count, friends fuel the fire of impulsive decision-making by siding with their friend. Not that this isn't appropriate at times, but they're friends, not counselors, pastors or domestic violence experts. Your circle of counsel and trust can include friends but shouldn't only be friends. Even if they're hard to find, know that there are gifted and good hearted experts that God has prepared to help you. If you're at a loss to find them, call us and we'll give you the names of some we trust.

Establish a Personal Trustworthy Circle of Support

Be selective on who you share with and who you ask to pray for your marriage. We have found it a good idea to pick individuals that know and like both of you. Don't select someone that is only friends with you or your spouse—they might have trouble remaining neutral. We have seen many "so called" friends give unhealthy advice to a couple to separate or divorce when it was what they wanted, not what the hurting spouse wanted.

Discuss together with your spouse who you will trust. We suggest that it be individuals or couples that are pro-marriage and willing to believe for a miracle for your marriage by supporting and praying for you. This is sometimes a pretty small group of people. Not everyone needs to know that you are struggling or the content of your struggles.

One important criterion to use is to consider whether or not the person(s) takes prayer seriously. Do they regularly try to hear God and are they careful to offer His wisdom and counsel and not just their own?

This is a litmus test we apply to persons we invite into our circle of trust for our own marriage. Do they trust God more than themselves? Do they have a history of reticence in responding to your questions or requests for advice because they "need to pray about it"? We are more likely to trust people who talk to and listen to God with us and for us than those who only respond from their own minds. Be serious about intercessory prayer. Ask these folks to pray for you to cultivate the heart of Jesus and to have the gift of faith to vision for the marriage that God wants you to have.

Be careful who you tell or you'll spend a lot of energy answering inquiries and sorting through or fending off negative counsel.

Try to Believe the Best

Assumptions about motives are lethal to relationships. Most of us are capable of constructing elaborate explanations for the way our spouse said something, did something, etc. Some of us are more prone to this type of paranoia than others due to past relational experiences in which we've been burned (e.g., used, betrayed, abandoned, etc.). We imagine the worst case scenario to psychologically prepare our hearts for rejection, neglect and abandonment. Obviously, such imaginative scenarios are sometimes based in reality, but they are often unfounded.

It's a risk to try to believe the best about your partner because it may not be true, and you may get hurt. But it leads to great possibilities for your partner and your relationship. Think about how you feel toward someone who believes in you. Who is it? How do you behave toward them? Do you try to live up to their expectations?

Remember that the core of the coaching approach is to practice the discipline of believing in others. This is based on the faith walk of Jesus who died for us while we were still sinners, wholeheartedly believing in the people we would become and be once we accepted his gift of redemption. In other words, he believed in us enough to die for us when it was unreasonable to do so; the just for the unjust, the sinless one for sinners. Thus when we believe the best about our partner, we walk in the faith footsteps of Jesus for whom our partners will become as we believe the best about them.

Enthusiastic Agreement

When you view your marriage as the object of your efforts in coaching, it is imperative that both participants fully support each other to voice their concerns and desires. We say it like this, *"If something is a problem for one of you, then it's a problem for the other because it's a problem for the relationship. And vice versa. You see, marriage isn't about the needs of one partner being greater than the other, but the needs of both being the concern and responsibility of each other."*

This principle clearly reflects an egalitarian model of marriage that esteems the needs and desires of both partners and which requires mutual submission. In simple terms it means that partners take turns having things their way when they don't agree on things.

Bill Harley, author of *His Needs Her Needs,* gets credit for this principle. When you are involved in a significant season of conflict in your marriage and/or when you are in the midst of repairs and healing, don't do anything that your partner doesn't enthusiastically endorse. You may think that is extremely impractical. Well, it might be difficult, but it is effective in forcing conflicted couples into discussions about their desires, and it puts a premium on patience in the process of negotiation.

We practice this to prevent misunderstandings and to proactively strengthen our team of two by asking each other for one another's support, not each other's permission. It goes like this, *"I'd love to go for a bike ride with some friends Saturday afternoon for about two hours. Would you support that? Sure Jeff, I would love for you to do that. I know how much you enjoy that. I'll look forward to dinner with you and maybe a movie?"* Notice that I didn't ask for permission. That's a pet peeve for us in our relationship and the relationships we coach because permission language can set up one partner to behave as a parent and the other as a child, and that interferes with the goal of both partners having the same status as adults in the marriage.

Never, Ever give up!

Fighting for your marriage may be the hardest thing you ever do. But, never stop striving, straining, studying, trying, praying, journaling, reading, etc. when it comes to your marriage. You made vows that are pretty serious and very demanding; for better for worse, for richer or poorer, in sickness and in health, *till death do us part.*

If you were fighting a deadly disease you would use all of your resources and search diligently for a cure that could save or prolong your life. Why should saving your marriage be any different! In our experience people give up too soon, stop trying because they can't see beyond the dissension, stop trying and rush towards closure in order to move on and away from the relational pain. What is the hurry? If your spouse is not willing to try right now, waiting will not make anything worse. Use that time to work on yourself and your relationship with God. Do what YOU can do.

At some point it will probably be way beyond your strength, will, intelligence and other resources to try in your marriage. That's by design. God wants us to have to depend on Him. Take heart, Christ has overcome the world! When you come to the end of yourself you can decide to come to the beginning of Him who is the author and sustainer of relationships! He is the one who has victory over death which is more than adequate power to prevent your relationship from dying and if necessary, to resurrect it from the dead! And in Him all things hold together. Let Him hold you together.

Take Time to Study

Now that you're equipped for your crisis, look for time to thoroughly absorb the rest of the book. You'll find the key ingredients you need to continue the healing process and to continue strengthening and protecting your marriage during the process of recovery and into the future. Let the crisis be a lesson and a motivator to change. The best defense against the demise of your marriage is a good offense using the essential elements of Christian Marriage Coaching: Heart, Hope and Skill. Be encouraged that every page you read, every concept you grasp and every skill you refine by using it regularly are the nutrients you need on a daily basis to build and sustain a hopeful, pleasurable and purposeful marriage.

BONUS CHAPTER
Reflection Questions:

1. How has this chapter inspired you?

_____

_____

_____

_____

_____

2. What are the key tips that you needed to hear?

_____

_____

_____

_____

_____

3. What options do you see and what are you motivated to do in your crisis after reading this?

_____

_____

_____

_____

_____

Appendices

APPENDIX A: Time-Out for Marriage Moments

Most couples have heated moments and challenging conversations. Jill and I jokingly refer to these as 'marriage moments,' but often they aren't funny. Feelings get hurt and sometimes days of silence ensue. It only takes a few moments to do damage that takes a long time to fix. You know the drill, right?

We continue to learn that a simple time-out during a precarious conversation is often all that's needed to get perspective and gain control of emotions. Agreed breaks in conversation ranging from five minutes to a day help us to put ourselves in position to hear each other's honest thoughts and feelings in a way that builds our relationship instead of eroding it. Wisdom in relationships is evident by restraint when it comes to words.[91]

Time-outs in sports serve several functions. They provide a 'breather' when participants become fatigued, a break from fast-paced action to consider strategy, and they interrupt momentum so things don't get out of hand. Time-outs in conversation provide opportunity for participants to rejuvenate, to change perspective and to calm emotions so that reason can prevail.

To use time-outs as a proactive strategy to have great conversations:
1. Agree with your partner about how to use them.
2. Agree that either of you can ask for time-out.
3. Decide at the point of time-out how long it will be.
4. Use time-out to pray, reflect and journal to emote and get perspective.
5. Reconvene at the agreed time.

The wise use of time-outs sometimes factors in the outcome of athletic contests. Few experienced competitors fail to use their allotted time-outs because they understand their value. We see experienced couples using them effectively to create more great conversations that don't get derailed by upset emotions or careless words.

APPENDIX B: Typical Progression in Marriage Coaching

In our experience, many couples face the common challenge of discomfort and displeasure in their relationship. Whether in our own marriage or helping other couple, we've found that a step-wise process which emphasizes skills is an efficient way to reduce discomfort and increase pleasure in the relationship.[92]

1. The couple feels uncomfortable about their relationship.
2. They would both like things to be different, but they're unsure how to change things.
3. They report frustration in their attempts to communicate about their wants and needs.
4. They would ideally like to eventually solve their problems themselves.
5. They love the idea of learning skills that they can use on their own.
6. They've never heard of a skills approach to marriage.
7. They are quick learners of skills and exercises to strengthen their marriage.
8. They leave our sessions feeling hopeful about the progress they are making.[93]
9. They report in the following session that they didn't use the skill(s) we taught them.
10. We trouble-shoot the break-down and encourage them to recommit to having conversations in a better and different way. We remind them, ***"If you can't have the conversation in a good way, don't have the conversation."***
11. We re-teach and re-facilitate a conversation in our presence.

12. Their confidence grows to be able to use the skill and/or do the exercise on their own.

13. They are better able to use key aspects of the skill that helped them to have productive conversation.

14. They leave the session with renewed hope.

15. They call, write or report in the next session that they did better on their own.[94]

16. We keep teaching and facilitating use of skills and exercises. We continue a collaborative style of coaching by continuing to ask the couple what else they need. An effective question that helps couples to articulate what they need is, *"If you could custom create a tool to accomplish something important for your marriage, what would the tool would do?"*

17. The couple continues to work the process at home during times they protect for their marriage.

18. The frequency of our appointments together decreases as they experience improvement in their ability to coach their own marriage (i.e., A couple's ability to collaborate in discerning what their marriage needs, and then planning to meet those needs by choosing skills and exercises to help them communicate, resolve conflict, build closeness, etc.).

19. They tell us that they think they are done for now with Marriage Coaching and want to know if they can come back for a "tune-up" in the future. We say *"Yes"*.

20. We ask them to review the daily, weekly, monthly recipe of the ingredients they need to keep what they gained; the amount of time they need to spend together and how to spend it together. At this point they are usually very clear about what they need to do, and they say, *"We just need to do it"*.

21. We urge them to consider how they can give to others what they have gained for themselves. We point out that this is God's way of multiplying ministry, by giving to us and then opening the door for us to help others. We encourage couples to give to others to help them to stay fresh and sharp with their skills.

The Progression of Coaching Your Own Marriage

We detailed the progression of a typical Marriage Coaching situation to alert you to the indicators of progress as you coach your own marriage. At first you may feel awkward and you may stumble. Learning this skill is not unlike learning to ride a bike, a skateboard or to swing a golf club. You start as a beginner and through **practice** become proficient. Notice the emphasis on the word **practice!** How do you integrate any skill into your life in a way that it becomes a habit? **PRACTICE.**

Let's pause to reflect for a few minutes. Consider the typical process (steps #1 - #21). Now, reflect on Bill and Marilyn's conversation in chapter 5. And finally, review the steps to coach your own marriage.

APPENDIX C: Discover the Desires of Your Heart/Their Heart

What thoughts have you been having about your marriage?

(Example: I've been thinking that we have a pretty good marriage and that it is important to not take that for granted. We've seen too many couples who report that they became lax and that they stopped working on their marriage by not making time for dates, conversation or recreation. I've been thinking that doing more fun things together would be good for us.)

_____
_____
_____
_____
_____
_____
_____
_____
_____

What has been the biggest feeling you've had recently about your marriage?

*(Example: I've been feeling **grateful** and **sad**; grateful that we've survived some very challenging circumstances, and that we haven't given up on essential practices, like forgiveness, recommitment and open sharing about honest feelings, even when those feelings have been unpleasant. I've been feeling sad about things I've done and said that have caused pain because I realize that we have a limited number of days. I don't want to waste the gift of life with pain or regret.)*

_____

_____

_____

_____

_____

_____

_____

_____

What do you want in regard to communication, conflict resolution, affection?

*(Example: In regard to **communication**, I want to more regularly hear and say things we appreciate about each other. In regard to **conflict**, I want to be more patient to hear your perspective when we are conflicted. Regarding **affection**, I want to receive more spontaneous gestures of affection like hugs.)*

_____

_____

_____

_____

_____

_____

APPENDIX D: Covenant for Our Shared Goal

Date: _____

Participants:_____

Goal: _____

_____

_____

_____

_____

_____

Purpose:_____

_____

_____

_____

_____

_____

Desires (What it will mean to us to accomplish this goal):

_____

_____

_____

_____

_____

What you can count on from me (husband or wife):

_____

_____

_____

_____

_____

The SEA I would like from you:

_____

_____

_____

_____

_____

_____

What you can count on from me (the opposite):

_____

_____

_____

_____

_____

_____

The SEA I would like from you:

_____

_____

_____

_____

_____

_____

Signatures:

_____

_____

APPENDIX E: SEA Exercise

Think of one or two goals/achievements you accomplished together.

1. _____
2. _____

List the people that provided support, beginning with your partner and including others (practical gestures that said they wanted you to succeed), and encouragement (words of encouragement about their belief in you, why your efforts are worth it), and accountability (reminders that you were born for this, and that you asked them to push you when the going got tough).

List of people and what they did and/or said.

1. _____
2. _____
3. _____
4. _____
5. _____

How do you feel as you think about the energy, efforts and courage of those who dared to believe in you, to sacrifice for you to fulfill your dreams and to walk toward your destiny? Can you imagine achieving your goal(s) without their support?

APPENDIX F: Great Communication in 15 Minutes a Day!

"It (love) always protects, always trusts, always hopes, always perseveres." (1 Corinthians 13:7; NIV)
Equity in relationships is built by *skillful* sharing of honest thoughts and feelings. Notice the accent on skill. This is because skill is imperative to keep things positive and safe. Sharing free-for-alls rarely go well, especially when emotions run high and the participants are flustered. The good news is that about anything can be shared with anyone, when it is done *skillfully* and in love. The bad news is that most of us have

room for improvement in the area of skill.

The hallmark of enduring relationships is perseverance. But, just because a relationship remains intact doesn't mean that it is pleasurable. That takes work, and skillful efforts raise the probability of an enduring relationship being pleasurable. Achieving this is not that difficult.

I can't name one couple that hasn't benefited from regular use of the tool called "The Daily Temperature Reading" combined with the skill of active listening. Partners that share the following five areas of information on a daily basis invariably report more pleasure and fewer misunderstandings in their relationship. All it takes is 10-15 minutes a day. Soon it is a habit, like any other self-care habit, that protects the health and pleasure of your relationship. Here are the five areas:

- **Appreciation**

    These can be anything you appreciate about your spouse or things that they did. Share as many as you can. Realize that you build credit in their love bank with these.

- **New Information**

    Share things that you learned while away from your spouse. Misunderstandings are prevented when we share essential information in a timely fashion.

- **Puzzles**

    These are internal or external mysteries. *I'm puzzled about why I've been so tired lately* or *I'm puzzled about why you didn't stop at the store on the way home like you promised.* Puzzles don't need to be answered, but could be if answering doesn't derail continuation of the exercise. Puzzles prompt us to confide things we are unsure about. Remember, confiding honest thoughts and feelings builds closeness.

- **Complaint with Request for Change**

    Say what you don't like and what you would like instead. Irritating things happen in any relationship. This is a way to bring those things up in an assertive way so that they don't fester. *"I don't like when you turn on the hallway light and leave the bedroom door open in the morning when you get up before I do, and I would like it if you could remember to turn off the light and close the door."* This is a good time to tell your partner what you heard them say in order to clarify their complaint. *"I heard you say it bothers you if I leave the light on and door open when you're still sleeping?"* Note: Heavier complaints should be said in other tools, not this one. The DTR is for everyday conversations, not highly emotional or complicated exchanges.

- **Wishes, Hopes and Dreams**
  Sharing hopes for the future is a great way to tie a bow on your time of sharing. This helps you to look forward to a positive future together. When we know what our spouse wants, we can help to make it happen. *"I want to go on a date, just you and me, to have some fun and undistracted time together."*
  The content shared by any couple is obviously different, but the process is similar. Feel free to share as many or few items as come to mind in each area.

Prayer

Lord, please give us desire and hope to keep trying to make our relation-ships what they can be when centered in you. Please embolden and equip us to try, and empower us with your hopeful and strong heart. In Jesus' name. Amen.

Note: Virginia Satir was the first to package five areas of information important to share in any relationship. The PAIRS Foundation packaged this exercise as "The Daily Temperature Reading," See, www.pairs.com, or http://www.smartmarriages.com/tempreading.html

If You Want More

For additional information on marriage coaches, counselors and upcoming seminars for marriages, go to our website, www.graceandtruthrelationship.com, or write to Jeff at jeff.gtre@gmail.com or Jill at jill.gtre@gmail.com.

For information on Marriage Coach training visit www.greatrelationships.org. Note that this is a non-profit organization designed to train as many couples as possible in Marriage Coaching, globally.

And, don't forget the endnotes. There are numerous books, websites, names of colleagues and their ministries mentioned in the endnotes.

Endnotes

1. Tony Stoltzfus, www.coach22.com.
2. Richard and Sharon's ministry is Stubborn Pursuits, Inc. Reach them at www.stubbornpursuits.wordpress.com
3. What about situations when one of you is willing to work and the other isn't (yet). We would encourage you with the words of Danny Silk, www.lovingonpurpose.com. "The moment you take responsibility for your part of the relationship, the relationship will begin to change."
4. The heart is the well-spring of life, and the source of our speech. Proverbs 4:23, Luke 6:45.
5. John 10:10 Jesus says, "The thief comes to steal, kill and destroy but I have come that you might have abundant life." Of course there will be seasons of struggle in marriage, but these should be relatively transient and not the prevailing characteristic of dynamic, growing marriages where both partners are constantly seeking and open to growth in their hearts and skills in a way that fuels hope and provides pleasure.
6. To our understanding, Bill Harley, author of His Needs Her Needs was the first to say this.
7. This is unethical behavior by a counselor. All decisions about a marriage belong to the couple, not the counselor. Professionals sometimes abuse their position and power by attempting to direct their clients lives based on their personal philosophies or biases. That's why it is essential that you understand the stance that your mentors, coaches and counselors take about marriage. Are they "Marriage Friendly"? Will they be the last person in the room to declare the marriage dead? Will they help you with your goals for your marriage if you want to strengthen, protect or to save it? Do

they believe that all decisions about your marriage belong to you? See www.marriagefriendlytherapists.com for more information. We don't know of a Christianized version of such an organization, so we applaud Bill Doherty for founding this organization that honors, esteems and fights for marriage.

8. It would take another five years to develop through Jill's input and practice in our own marriage and with couples who came to us asking for help.

9. Synonyms for good-will include heart, faith, hope, selflessness, respect, etc. Anything that expresses the notion that a person is doing the best for the marriage is good-will. Faith-based persons often muster this up and sustain it through their spiritual beliefs, including their relationship with God.

10. The repository of effective relationship education curriculum has been gathered and promoted globally by The Coalition for Couples Education, otherwise known as Smart Marriages. The founder and proponent, Diane Solee continues as a tireless and passionate champion and promoter of all that is healthy and good for the establishment, growth and sustenance of healthy marriage and family relationships. See www.smartmarriages.com, and don't miss the daily newsletter to keep pace with this body of information. In addition, a new organization, NARME, www.narme.net, National Association for Relationship and Marriage Education, has been formed to complement the work being done through Smart Marriages.

11. Jill and I have taught live seminars, conducted tele-classes, and provided Marriage Coaching to couples all over the U.S., India, China, Thailand, Brazil and Canada. Many of our students have taken what we have taught and modeled to marriages in multiple other countries.

12. Learning begins with unconscious incompetence: We don't know that we don't know. Next is conscious incompetence: We know that we don't know. Enlightenment begins as we learn, but use of skills requires conscious effort. Finally, is unconscious competence:

We integrate new learning into our habits and new thoughts and behaviors become second nature.

13. Many couples have "joked" that they need to take us home to coach them through their conversations at home. Why? They're saying that having witnesses to their conversations helps them to "behave," and that the way we facilitate their asking and listening helps them to hear each other in a better way. Thus, our end goal in coaching is to help couples to eventually do for themselves what we initially do for them; structuring the conversation in a way that they are both able to share and hear each other's honest thoughts, feeling and desires.

14. Couples who can benefit from Marriage Coaching include the full continuum of types of relationships; couples considering engagement, ones already engaged, newlyweds, married couples wanting more pleasure, closeness or to resolve conflict, and couples in crisis who are separated or headed for divorce. The basic process of coaching is the same regardless of the content of a couple's situation.

15. Tony Stoltzfus' seminal book, Leadership Coaching, comprehensively articulates the necessary disciplines, skills, values and heart of a Christian coach. Go to www.coach22.com to read the first chapter and to order your copy.

16. The application of coaching to parenting or other personal relationships (friendship, work, etc.) is beyond the scope of this book. However, some of these skills and exercises can be adapted for use in any relationship. A great book on the application of coaching in parenting is by Greg Bland, Co-Active Parent Coaching, available at www.coach22.com.

17. Marriage Resource Center of the Miami Valley: www.marriageresourcecenter.org.

18. LifeForming Leadership Coaching, www.lifeformingcoach.org.

19. We worked together with the couples and the Church for two intensive weeks. Miraculously, both marriages survived, and the church had peace and gratitude about the outcome.

20. "People are responsible for their own lives," Tony Stoltzfus, Leadership Coaching, www.coach22.com.

21. Many couples we've coached complain that unsolicited advice from a counselor has damaged their relationship.

22. While an individual male or female coach can be effective, our passion is to train couples as teams of two.

23. Jill and I won't coach a couple unless they are agreeable to being coached as a couple (we view their marriage as the client). We do offer adjunct individual sessions, but only if the couple's sessions continue.

24. It is important to make a distinction between levels or degrees of healing. While coaching is best for people who demonstrate a high level of adaptive functioning (e.g. work, school, relationships), and counseling is the method of choice for those whose adaptive functioning is compromised (i.e., not functioning on par with their abilities, or there has been a significant and lasting downturn in their work, school, relationships), the reality is that if a couple is motivated to grow and change they can benefit from a coaching approach even if their functioning is compromised. They may need an additional or supplementary approach such as counseling, or they may not. We've seen highly compromised marriages recover quickly and thoroughly by embracing the skills and process and using it diligently.

25. It is extremely important for Marriage Coaching couples and couples being coached to understand the scope and boundaries of this approach, so the ethics of this approach is covered in our Marriage Coaching training program.

26. Again, other approaches may be needed, but at some point outside assistance will end and a couple will be alone to privately imple-ment what they have learned. This is the promise and possibility of couples coaching their own marriage; they work on their marriage while also participating in it. A good analogy is small business development. The founder(s) work on the business and in the business. Business owners regularly take a step back to ask what

the business needs while also putting their shoulder to the plow to work in the business to provide what the business needs.

27. "Now faith is confidence in what we hope for and assurance about what we do not see..." (Hebrews 11:1)

28. Definition of Church: The Body of Christ across denominations that gathers in a variety of ways in a variety of places, including but not limited to "Church" buildings.

29. Approaches to relationships that facilitate honest sharing between partners are contraindicated when spousal abuse/domestic violence is present in a relationship. Disclosure of honest thoughts and feelings to an abusive partner can result in reprisal. Assistance from a professional counselor trained to help couples to change abusive behavior patterns is more appropriate than Marriage Coaching when such issues are disclosed by a couple or discovered during the coaching process. www.domesticviolence.org is a good resource, as is http://www.ndvh.org (this is a hotline).

30. Couples can impart to others what they have learned through coaching or reading in an informal way, but some couples may want to receive formal training and to coach other couples and perhaps train other couples as part of their ministry or professionally for a fee. If that is your interest, please contact us to explore training options.

31. I first heard this from Rick Marks, who confirmed (email correspondence Sept. 21, 2009), that the concept is unique to him, although he first heard a related concept that was seminal for his own thinking from Terry Hargrave who spoke about his book, The Essential Humility of Marriage, www.terryhargrave.com/6. in 1999 at the Denver SmartMarriages conference. Rick Marks can be reached at Richard Marks, PhD, Enriched Relationships, 904-724-8683 and www.marriageforlife.org and www.enrichedrelationships.com.

32. This is a commitment to do right things and best things for the marriage regardless of how we are feeling toward our partner.

33. "...the Son of Man did not come to be served, but to serve, and to give his life as a ransom for many." (Matthew 20:28)

34. Read I Corinthians 13 and ask yourself if love characterizes your conversations.
35. Taking a walk together works well for us. It eliminates distractions, and depending on the route we choose, we can closely estimate the amount of time we'll have to focus on our conversation. No phones, no kids, no computers, etc.
36. A Great Book about this concept, Energy Management is "The Power of Full Engagement", Jim Loehr and Tony Schwartz.
37. 89% of 165 couples were still married three years after we coached them.
38. We facilitated Thelma confronting George about his half-hearted engagement of the process, and supported her goal of living above reproach as much as possible so George wouldn't be able to blame his half-hearted efforts on her. Thelma had a clear conscience about her efforts, even though she said it was the hardest thing she'd ever done to not play on his level. Somehow, they are still together today! This is a good illustration of Winston Churchill's life maxim to "Never, never, never, never ever, ever, ever give up."
39. "Now faith is being sure of what we hope for..."
40. What can you do if only one of you wants to work on your marriage? Marriage 911 and www.reconcilinggodsway.com provide a workbook that one partner can go through with the support of a same-sex peer to focus on their own thinking, behavior and relationship with God. Also, Stubborn Pursuits is a ministry founded by a couple that successfully reconciled their marriage after a long separation. They provide coaching to individual men and women who want to save their marriage, www.stubbornpursuits.wordpress.com.
41. There has been a lot of discussion and writing about the unhealthiness of losing one's identity in marriage. This is not what we are suggesting, but rather that there is something unique about the synergistic combination of the gifts, strengths and passions of two individuals that in fact supersedes those of either partner.
42. The number one answer to this question is "More fun". Many couples report that they become so involved in career, raising

children, hobbies, etc., that they stop having fun together. Other highly ranked answers include better communication, more physical affection and intimacy, and more time to talk. The number one answer for conflicted couples is a better way to discuss and resolve conflicts.

43. To my awareness, Stephen Covey popularized this principle through his book, "Seven Habits of Highly Effective People."

44. One such group is A Fellowship of Christian Marriage and Family Coaches. We communicate about our own marriages and things we've learned to help other couples on the private Facebook group page. Please request membership if you are interested. In addition, marriage mentoring ministries in churches and community marriage resource centers are good places to look for information and for other couples who have a wealth of ideas and resources that you might find helpful.

45. Some action-steps will be recurring, such as choosing to take a walk after dinner three nights a week to share new information with each other, or starting the day with conversation and prayer three mornings a week.

46. "…just as the Son of Man did not come to be served, but to serve, and to give his life as a ransom for many." (Matthew 20:28).

47. See I Corinthians 13

48. The concepts, attitudes and skills of holding your spouse's heart can be applied to other relationships. For information on applying coaching skills to parenting see the Family Coaching section of www.christiancoachingcenter.org.

49. Tony Stoltzfus sees a progression from skill to discipline to heart. He says that skills practiced consistently become a discipline and disciplines work their way into our hearts to become part of us, Leadership Coaching: The Disciplines, Skills and Heart of a Coach, www.coach22.com.

50. Level I Marriage Coaching training begins with Effective Listening. For more information, write to Jeff at jeff.gtre@gmail.com, or jill.gtre@gmail.com or visit, www.graceandtruthrelationship.

com or www.greatrelationships.org. Seminars on How to Coach Your Own Marriage or How to Coach Your Marriage through Emotional and Difficult Conversations are done through our direct service Counseling and Coaching practice, Grace and Truth Counseling and Coaching. Training of couples to coach other couples is done through the not for profit organization we started, Great Relationships.

51. This means that the facilitation of healing, strengthening and protection of their marriage relationship, not either individual, is the objective of our efforts.

52. See He Walked Among Us, Paul Miller.

53. Definition of compassion from www.merriamwebster.com.

54. In John 11:35 Jesus wept in response to the news about his friend Lazarus' death. He felt compassion and then behaved with compassion by raising Lazarus from being dead.

55. An excellent resource for coaching questions is Coaching Questions, by Tony Stoltzfus, www.coach22.com

56. We're no longer surprised because we've seen it happen so often. While we do pre-plan coaching and training sessions by noting the issues we anticipate to come up, we remain poised to seize teachable moments with coaching students and to follow couples we are coaching where their hearts lead them. Making room for them to lead and God to work in the situation has been essential for transformation to take place. Some of the growth and change we've witnessed would have certainly been crowded out if we had arrived to coaching and teaching opportunities with a strict script of questions that we needed to be answered during the session.

57. Their reference is to the award-winning movie The Wizard of Oz. Remember when Dorothy finally arrives at the Emerald City, gains an audience with the great wizard and sees behind the curtain— learning how the Wizard was making things happen in Oz?

58. Author of the best-selling book, His Needs, Her Needs. Willard F. Harley, Jr. ©1986, 1994, 2001 by Willard F. Harley, Jr. (Published by Fleming H. Revel, Grand Rapids, MI 49516).

59. We continue to discover different ways to use it. "What do you want for the weekend?" "What do you want to do this evening?" "What do you want regarding our marriage?"

60. Philippians 2:3, "Do nothing out of selfish ambition or vain conceit, but . . ."

61. Philippians 1:6; II Peter 1:5-11

62. I Corinthians 13:4-7

63. Here are a couple of questions to consider if you want to drill down on these two areas: "On a scale of 1-10, how comfortable are you being open about your honest feelings with your spouse? Support your answer. What would you like more of or less of that would help you to feel more comfortable and safe to share your honest feelings?" Regarding physical intimacy; "On a scale of 1-10, how satisfied are you with the frequency and quality of your lovemaking? What is happening that you are happy about, and what would you like more of or to start happening?"

64. Philippians 2:13, "for it is God who works in you to will and to act in order to fulfill his good purpose."

65. The end of this story is that my stance gave her pause to consider another way to handle her sexuality. She decided to abstain from sex outside of marriage, and to recover from the multiple intimate attachments she'd made with other men in her past. Years later she called to say she was happily married, and that issues with intimacy had been resolved.

66. We assert that it is common because many couples we've seen for coaching and in seminars tell us that they tried counseling but all they did was to talk about their problems. The majority weren't equipped with skills to build closeness by communicating to reach shared understanding or to resolve emotionally charged conflicts, or to set shared goals to accomplish something important to both of them for their relationship.

67. Margaret and Jim helped each other throughout the process to vent angry, sad, scared, and glad feelings to diffuse emotion before they tried to have rational and productive conversations. First, Margaret

repeatedly asked Jim about his feelings and didn't respond with her opinions or her own feelings. Then, Jim did the same for Margaret as a controlled and safe way for them to share their honest feelings in a way that eventually de-escalated strong emotions that were interfering with a rational discussion.

68. If you're curious, it was the infamous P90X® program. www.beachbody.com

69. Richard and Sharon Wildman, www.stubbornpursuits.wordpress.com

70. Tony Stoltzfus, www.coach22.com

71. Guess who? My bride; Jill Williams.

72. Leadership Coaching, Peer Coaching, www.coach22.com

73. Our observation has been that couples who serve others are under special spiritual pressure. This has been severe enough in our own marriage and others we've trained that we suggest development of an intercessory prayer team to support your marriage, and training for marriage ministry before you begin training others.

74. Marriage Coaching continues to be reviewed as simple, practical, clear and culturally transferable by couples we've served from every major world culture; Asian, S. Asian, European, South American, African, Australian, North American and the Far East. Christian marriages from each of these cultures aspire to achieve shared understanding of one another's thoughts, feelings and desires. All realize that God consistently focuses their attention on areas of growth and change for more loving attitudes and practices in their marriage, and all have reported significant breakthroughs and progress in understanding each other and experiencing healthy and pleasurable emotional and physical intimacy through opening and holding each other's hearts with skillful loving respect.

75. This principle was discovered during the war in the Falkland Islands. Temperatures were very low. Soldiers who suffered wounds that would have usually been mortal survived. This serendipitous discovery was quickly applied in emergency medicine.

76. I developed this exercise in the 1990s while working with youth

in a mental health day treatment program. In addition to glad, I added proud. I assigned this to youth to help them to vent their strong emotions in words instead of through their behavior, and to become more emotionally literate (i.e., capable of identifying and expressing their feelings). PAIRS ®, www.pairs.com packaged this exercise as Emptying the Emotional Jug.

77. Credit for this analogy goes to Rich Wildman, www.stubbornpursuits.wordpress.com.

78. In case you find this difficult to do from the written description and option is to have a session or two to learn this exercise from trained facilitators. It's one of the most important exercises in our repertoire of exercises for our own marriage and to help other couples.

79. Laugh Your Way to a Better Marriage, www.laughyourway.com. This paraphrase is from his live seminar, which we highly recommend. Get it on DVD from the website.

80. August 2005 in Bradenton/Sarasota, Florida. Sponsored by www.marriagesavers.org for Marriage Savers of the Sun Coast®

81. www.stubbornpursuits.wordpress.com

82. Uncommon Therapy, by Jay Haley Norton, W. W. & Company, Inc. April 1993

83. II Corinthians 12:9

84. Again, mutually meeting each other's needs in a relationship is excellent marriage insurance. See Dr. Bill Harley's best-seller, "His Needs, Her Needs" for details.

85. Superb materials for a marriage crisis are Marriage 911, also known as Reconciling God's Way. Find details on these at http://nationalmarriage.com/marriage-911-first-response.html or http://www.reconcilinggodsway.org/

86. Obviously, this is an extremely complex and controversial topic; so much so that I'm not going to attempt to thoroughly discuss it here.

87. Steve Grissom produced a video series "Before You Divorce" and curriculum for Divorce Care groups (which have a reconciliation emphasis) for just this reason; to educate persons considering divorce about the innumerable consequences to them and others.

Go to www.divorcecare.org for more information.

88. How to structure a separation is beyond the scope of this book. And, if things are that severe, you will probably need professional guidance from a counselor with experience in such situations. You can call or write to us for referrals if this is what you need.

89. The privacy and lack of built in accountability of living alone instead of having one's spouse present can make it too easy to self-medicate emotional pain (substance use, pornography), to indulge a self-serving lifestyle that takes on a life of its own, or to cultivate another intimate relationship. All of these interfere with a return to a committed and interdependent lifestyle of marriage. The best use of a structured separation is toward the goal of reconciliation and includes accountability. We once housed a man for three months while separated from his wife. Our mere presence provided accountability to him for his activities during this period of life.

90. PLEASE get good help with this. Good means a marriage friendly counselor or coaching couple who believes for and will honor your desire to reconcile. Believe it or not there are humanistic secular counselors that regularly execute marriages by proclaiming the hopelessness of a marital situation. They use their position and power to recommend separation with intent to divorce. Again, we will reiterate that we too believe that there are some circumstances that justify divorce, but as a rule, if a couple wants to reconcile then who is the counselor or Marriage Coaching couple to suggest otherwise?

91. Proverbs 10:19 and 17:27.

92. Keep in mind that the average amount of time we spend with couples from start to finish is 12-15 hours total over a 3-4 month period. Of course these numbers vary with the content that couples are working on. Obviously the more complex, painful or challenging, the more time needed.

93. Typical comments are, "We were able to talk today in a way we are rarely able to communicate," and "We've never been able to

talk like this. Can you come live with us?" (They assume that they will always need us to coach their process.)

94. Their unconscious incompetence, not knowing how to do differently, moves to conscious competence. They know what to do and they do it well as long as they are thinking about what to do and when. (This was where Tony and Nikki were in the learning process when they coached their marriage on their vacation.)

CPSIA information can be obtained
at www.ICGtesting.com
Printed in the USA
LVOW10s1928061017
551488LV00007B/718/P